FILM STARS

Stars are an integral part of every major film industry in the world. In this pivotal new series, each book is devoted to an international movie star, looking at the development of their identity, their acting and performance methods, the cultural significance of their work, and their influence and legacy. Taking a wide range of different stars, including Mickey Rourke, Brigitte Bardot and Amitabh Bachchan among others, this series encompasses the sphere of silent and sound acting, Hollywood and non-Hollywood areas of cinema, and child and adult forms of stardom. With its broad range, but a focus throughout on the national and historical dimensions to film, the series offers students and researchers a new approach to studying film.

SERIES EDITORS

Martin Shingler and Susan Smith

George CLOONEY

PAUL MCDONALD

THE BRITISH FILM INSTITUTE
Bloomsbury Publishing Plc
50 Bedford Square, London, WC1B 3DP, UK
1385 Broadway, New York, NY 10018, USA

BLOOMSBURY is a trademark of Bloomsbury Publishing Plc

First published in Great Britain 2019 by Bloomsbury on behalf of the British
Film Institute
Reprinted 2019
21 Stephen Street, London W1T 1LN
www.bfi.org.uk

The BFI is the lead organisation for film in the UK and the distributor of
Lottery funds for film. Our mission is to ensure that film is central to our
cultural life, in particular by supporting and nurturing the next generation of
film-makers and audiences. We serve a public role which covers the cultural,
creative and economic aspects of film in the UK.

A catalogue record for this book is available from the British Library.

A catalog record for this book is available from the Library of Congress.

ISBN: HB: 978-1-9112-3992-5
           PB: 978-1-8445-7494-0
          ePDF: 978-1-9112-3932-1
         eBook: 978-1-9112-3933-8

Series: Film Stars

Typeset by Integra Software Services Pvt. Ltd.
Printed and bound in Great Britain

To find out more about our authors and books visit www.bloomsbury.com
and sign up for our newsletters.

CONTENTS

ACKNOWLEDGEMENTS

To the series editors Martin Shingler and Susan Smith, my gratitude not only for inviting me to contribute to this excellent collection of books but also for your patience in putting up with my delay in getting this book completed. To Tamar, my thanks for her love and support throughout every moment of working on the book, including our many conversations about the 'last movie star'. This book is dedicated to the memory of my mother.

INTRODUCTION: CLOONEY AND MODERN HOLLYWOOD

George Clooney is a distinct figure in modern Hollywood. After his film career took off in the mid-1990s, Clooney went on to star in a run of movies where he presented something quite different from his leading-man peers. By 2000, one commentator was noting Clooney

has emerged as the most unassailably regular, hetero leading guy in the business. Clooney – in his roles and in his life – is a man's man, without being too over-the-top (like [Arnold] Schwarzenegger or [Sylvester] Stallone), too sensitive ([Tom] Hanks), too outré ([Kevin] Spacey), or too boy toy ([Brad] Pitt, [Tom] Cruise). He's already being compared to Clark Gable and Cary Grant for his lethal combination of elegance and virility, without any great suggestion of depth (or Brando-ish, Bogart-ish darkness). He's more likable than Bruce Willis, less neurotic than Russell Crowe.

(DePaulo 2000: 186–7)

Instead of the inflated 'musculinity' of action stars Schwarzenegger, Stallone or Willis, the adult-boyishness of Cruise and Pitt, or the vulnerable everymanness of Hanks, Clooney embodied a version of masculinity that is handsome, cool, suave, charming, smooth, mature and elegantly styled. As his movie career continued, these meanings endured, becoming the qualities that Clooney was readily associated with not only on-screen but off-screen as well.

Widespread references in celebrity reporting to Clooney's looks and manner framed him as a definition of male desirability for the late twentieth and early twenty-first centuries. *People* magazine twice awarded him their annual 'The Sexiest Man Alive' award (Sanz 1997 and Leonard 2006). One magazine profile described him as 'the middleweight champion of charm' (Stein 2004). Another said: 'He's shrewd, he's virile, he's merry ... with the kind of good looks that evoke an interesting life instead of a blank state' (Carson 2007: 116). For it's 'Gorgeous George' profile, the January 2005 edition of US men's magazine *Esquire* affirmed Clooney's status as a 'man's man' with a cover image of Clooney in T-shirt and chinos and holding a beer, accompanied by the main cover line 'The Meaning of Life: Let's go over to Clooney's, have a coupla these [pointing to the beer] and figure it all out'. Inside, however, the images that ran with the article showed Clooney consciously presenting himself in unflattering guises, including one of him wearing goofy teeth carved from orange rind. This is just one small example of how self-deprecating humour has both worked against, while also being the ultimate expression of, Clooney's masculine confidence. Knowing he has the looks, the manner, the clothes and the lifestyle, Clooney doesn't have to try and so has freely poked fun at himself. Self-reflection has become a feature of Clooney's image, for consistently he's appeared as the most acute commentator and honest critic of his own stardom.

This book approaches Clooney from two directions, one conceptual, the other historical. Like all stars in Hollywood, Clooney is both actor and asset. As a film and television actor, Clooney has brought a specific range of signs and meanings to the screen, and as these have circulated in media markets, so Clooney has become a marketable attraction. Combining these symbolic and economic effects, Clooney's stardom operates in a similar manner to that of a brand. Stars and brands are both commercial identities: neither is a commodity but both function as means for selling commodities. Any brand has its symbolic component, a set of signs and their associated meanings, and an economic component, the use of those signs and meanings to link a collection of products while differentiating these from those of competitors. It is this mixture of similarity with difference which sees stars functioning in ways analogous to brands. Any star is a distinct personality, uniting one collection of films while distinguishing these from films starring other actors. It is for this reason that stars have been important to the economics of popular film. No two films are identical, and while uniqueness may generate the curiosity necessary to motivate consumers towards paying for something they've never exactly seen before, at the same time it leaves audience demand uncertain and so produces risk. Stars offer just one means for the popular film commodity to negotiate the balance between risk and security: a star performance contributes to making a film seem unique or different, yet the presence of the star presents a perceptible point of saleable continuity between films. Branding theory frequently likens brands to people, using metaphors such as 'brand personality' or 'brand identity' to explain how brands communicate. Movie stardom flips that relationship, making the person into a brand, a collection of signs and meanings used to sell films (McDonald 2013: 42–9). Conceptually, this book therefore examines Clooney as a branded presence in contemporary Hollywood.

The book aims to place the Clooney brand historically in the industrial and market contexts of modern Hollywood. Focusing on singular personalities, Hollywood stardom celebrates exceptional individualism. What this approach obscures, however, is how stardom is a system, a set of industrially coordinated collective inputs for producing performers as exceptional individuals. Hollywood history frequently takes the period of the 1930s and 1940s to be the apotheosis of the star system. During those decades, as part of their overall control of the film industry in the US, a small number of major companies – 'the studios' – committed in-house resources to self-consciously craft marketable identities for actors, singers, comedians and dancers, then made good on their investments by retaining performers on long-term contracts so that they could appear in numerous films over several years. In these conditions stars were produced and controlled by the studios. From the 1950s onwards changes in the industry and market for Hollywood film necessitated dissolving this system. Performers were no longer retained long-term but instead were usually hired on single-picture deals. Due to these changes, it is sometimes presumed the star system disappeared; it didn't, it was merely reconfigured. As performers became freelance talent for hire, the production of stardom moved outside the major studios. Rather than a process internalized by the major corporate players in Hollywood, the production of stardom was externalized with independent stars relying on the services of agents, personal managers and attorneys to mould and steer their careers. Star performers also discovered their freelance status afforded newfound opportunities for extending the roles they played in the film business, becoming directors, producers and writers, and setting up their own production companies. With these changes the major studios did not cease to be influential in the production of stardom. As a concentrated cluster of companies continued to dominate the US film industry and markets for film at home and abroad, independent stars remained dependent on the majors to achieve the kinds of opportunity and exposure their status required. A 'post-studio' star system therefore persists in modern Hollywood, where much of the work involved with producing stars now takes place outside the majors, yet the centralizing power of those companies still holds sway over the business (McDonald 2000, 2013: 87–122).

Linking these conceptual and historical perspectives, the chapters that follow situate the Clooney brand within certain dynamic points of tension that shape the post-studio Hollywood star system. In part, the changes that Hollywood underwent from the 1950s onwards arose due to competition from the popularization of television as an entertainment medium. Television viewing came to surpass cinema-going as the more popular form of leisure pursuit, yet for many performers, working in television became merely a platform from which to launch film careers. Chapter 1 covers Clooney's movement from television to film stardom. Despite struggling for many years to establish a stable career in both television and film, five years on the hit television medical drama *ER* (1994–2009) provided Clooney with enough popular visibility for him to become a leading man in film. Although both are screen media, television and film construct quite different contexts for the production of fame, with the effect that movement between small and big screen is never frictionless. Fame achieved in one medium never simply translates to another and examples abound of successful TV actors who've failed to make it in film. This chapter sees Clooney's transition from television to film therefore as a process of legitimization through which he not only struggled to create a distinct branded identity but also strived to achieve credibility as a leading man in film.

Comparing stars to brands requires some elaboration. On-screen film stars enact characters by using their bodies and voices. Whereas other forms of brands announce their presence in the marketplace through the signifying vehicles of trademarked logos, memorable names, and catchy slogans or taglines, with the film star it is the body and voice that communicate branded distinctiveness. Star performance is therefore branded performance. Just as product brands differentiate and standardize goods, so the performances of star brands produce differences and similarities between films. It is the work of the actor to perform differences, representing particular characters in specific narrative circumstances. To function as saleable assets, however, stars must also always be visible as 'playing themselves' between roles. With a figure like Clooney, the branding tension between difference and similarity therefore appears in his dual status as actor and star. Chapter 2 analyses how those tensions materialize with Clooney's enactment of a branded presence in film. It first identifies the bodily and vocal markers that have made Clooney a distinctive performing figure in film, in other words the signs of 'Clooneyness'. Analyses of acting in *O Brother, Where Art Thou?* (2000) and *Ocean's Eleven* (2001) then explore how Clooney's use of two modes of performance have enacted differences and similarities between films. Both modes are important definers of the Clooney brand, although as the cool, smooth performance used in *Ocean's Eleven* became the most commercially successful of Clooney's characterizations, and therefore the most popularly known, it enacted what became the predominant definition of the brand.

Clooney exemplifies the workings of post-studio stardom. As a freelance star, he's enjoyed the liberty to move between films budgeted at multiple tiers of production investment aimed at either the popular or speciality markets. Acting was foundational to forming the Clooney brand but over time he found creative opportunities for extending that brand by collaborating in the running of his own production companies and taking on additional creative roles as director, producer and writer. Using the concept of 'flexible stardom' (McDonald 2017), Chapter 3 positions Clooney in the tension between independence and Hollywood. It explores the Clooney brand as a product of, and product in, the industry and market for Hollywood film. Working for the major Hollywood corporations, their 'Indiewood' specialized production–distribution subsidiaries, and genuine independents, Clooney's career has traversed the industrial space of contemporary American film. Yet this autonomy has operated in a context where Clooney's independence has been dependent on the handful of large diversified media and communication conglomerates that represent modern Hollywood. Analysis of Clooney's positioning in the film market takes production budgets, box office revenues, scale of release, and ratings classifications, as indicators for the valuing, popularity, visibility and accessibility of Clooney's films. Finally, the chapter outlines extensions of the Clooney brand with the multiplication of his creative and business roles.

Over time the Clooney brand has acquired political meanings. On-screen Clooney has acted in or directed, produced and written films with explicitly political content. Off-screen he has openly and proudly declared himself a liberal, becoming a contemporary emblem of the Hollywood Left. By highlighting and speaking out on many unpopular or neglected issues, Clooney has used his fame to both mediate and magnify politics. Entertainment and politics work by differing purposes and principles, and so when movie stars engage with politics, questions inevitably arise over their credibility as political representatives. With what authority can politicized movie stars speak of the issues they espouse? Can they bring about positive change? The final chapter therefore places the Clooney brand at the intersection of entertainment and politics. Taking the examples of *Three Kings* (1999) and *Syriana* (2005) it first considers Clooney's representation of politics on-screen. The main body of the chapter then deals with Clooney's off-screen politics, outlining his self-conscious reflections on the status of the star as political representative, together with the terms in which he's become a target for attacks by the conservative Right. Final sections of the chapter deal with how the Clooney brand has been variously positioned in relation to the politics of organized labour, party fundraising, and humanitarian causes.

This book is therefore concerned with how the Clooney brand has navigated dynamic tensions between television and film, actor and star, independence and Hollywood, and entertainment and politics. Although never the subject of any specific chapter, a further tension weaving its way throughout the book is between present and past. The meanings of the Clooney brand are interpenetrated by the aura of nostalgia that has surrounded him. Clooney is very much a figure of modern Hollywood yet multiple lines of association have formed between him and older Hollywood. Film reviewers and commentators have persistently likened Clooney to certain male stars from earlier periods in Hollywood history, in particular Cary

Grant and Clark Gable. When *From Dusk Till Dawn* (1996) was released, reviewers observed:

George Clooney, whose previous feature film credits include 'Return of the Killer Tomatoes,' goes from television stardom in 'E.R.' to another try at leading-man stature on the big screen. Not many television actors make the transition easily, but not many look this much like Cary Grant.

(Maslin 1996)

From the first scene, it is clear that the 'ER' sensation, who has made numerous forgettable pics in the past, has the looks, authority and action-film savvy to be a new Clark Gable or 'Mad Max'-mold Mel Gibson.

(McCarthy 1996a: 98)

With Clooney's next film role, opposite Michelle Pfeiffer in *One Fine Day* (1996), similar comparisons were drawn:

It's not hard to conjure up Rosalind Russell and Cary Grant or elements of such classics as 'His Girl Friday' or 'The Awful Truth' when viewing this smartly pedigreed movie.

(Byrge 1996: 9)

[Clooney]'s the rare major actor who, like Clark Gable, holds equal appeal for men and women.

(McCarthy 1996a)

For Renée Zellweger, Clooney's co-star in *Leatherheads* (2008), he fits with a different lineage.

Every once in a while you get the real good guy. You've got your Jimmy Stewart. You've got your Paul Newman. Now you've got your George Clooney.

(quoted in West 2007: 306)

As these associations proliferated and persisted, the past became ever present for the Clooney brand. As one 2013 profile of Clooney observed:

a lot of people … call George Clooney a throwback. He is a throwback to what they suppose was a different time that created a different kind of celebrity. A lot of people even call him the closest thing we have to Clark Gable, a mantle he has accepted to the extent that he replicated Gable's rhythms and timing for O Brother, Where Art Thou? and sports a Gablean 'stache in The Monuments Men. But there are a lot of throwbacks in this world. George Clooney is the only throwback who lives in Clark Gable's freaking house.[1]

(Junod 2013: 128)

Rather than reviving any specific figure from Hollywood's past, it might be more appropriate to think of Clooney as 'incarnat[ing] our muddled nostalgia for Hollywood's golden age … [for] there's something fairly synthetic about him – as if, assembled out of our notions of what classic stars were like, he's too much like any of them to be convincing as any of them' (Carson 2007: 116). Beyond Gable and Grant, Clooney's nostalgic aura creates a more generalized evocation of the past. With O Brother, Where Art Thou?, Confessions of a Dangerous Mind (2002), Good Night, and Good Luck (2005), The Good German (2006), Leatherheads and The Monuments Men (2014), he's appeared in films set during periods in twentieth-century history. Other Clooney films formed associations with the past of film: Hail, Caesar! (2016) takes 1950s Hollywood as a context for comedy, while Ocean's Eleven, Solaris (2002) and Welcome to Collinwood (2002) all remade features from earlier decades. This investment in the past has gone further with Clooney's involvements in projects that are not only set in the past but which also borrow the production techniques of a former era. Television production Fail Safe (2000) remade the Cold War feature film drama *Fail Safe* (1964) while using methods of live transmission from television's past. Likewise, post-World War II drama *The Good German* used obsolete production technologies and techniques. Then there are Clooney's contemporary movies that are reminiscent of the past: *Intolerable Cruelty* (2003) owes to the tradition of screwball comedy, popularized in the 1930s and early 1940s with defining performances from Gable and Grant, while the political drama *Syriana* (2006) and conspiracy drama *Michael Clayton* (2007) share the cynical post-Vietnam sensibilities of some 1970s thrillers. As a product of the post-studio system, Clooney is an independent star but the years he spent working for Warner Bros. on *ER* and the films he starred in for the studio strongly evoke the star–studio alignments of the earlier studio-controlled system. Finally, through his political allegiances, Clooney's membership of the Hollywood Left has placed him in a long tradition of liberal stars stretching back to the silent era (Ross 2011). A recurrent concern running through the book is therefore how retro-stardom has formed an essential element in the Clooney brand, for he is an actor who belongs to Hollywoods both present and past.

Note

1 Clooney's house in Studio City, Los Angeles, is a former residence of Gable.

1 CROSS-MEDIA STARDOM: TELEVISION/FILM

At the start of his acting career, Clooney spent over a decade juxtaposing television and film assignments, working regularly in both media but achieving no success in either. This career phase came to an end when Clooney worked on the first five seasons of the television medical drama *ER* (1994–2009). Through *ER*, Clooney received widespread media attention and award-winning recognition. At the same time, during those years, Clooney also established his credentials as a leading man in film, so that by the time he left *ER*, he was then able to build and consolidate his status as a film star. Viewed in retrospect from the vantage point of knowing Clooney achieved film stardom, the transition from television to film might be regarded as just a stepping-stone on an inevitable path to movie stardom. For post-studio Hollywood stardom, however, television has acted as both platform and obstacle to film fame. Like Clooney, Clint Eastwood, Burt Reynolds, Michael J. Fox, Denzel Washington, Bruce Willis, Robin Williams, Tom Hanks, Jim Carrey, Brad Pitt and Will Smith are just some of the male actors who've become bankable film names on the back of television careers (McDonald 2013: 116–18). These successes mask, though, the problems of this transition. There is no certainty that television fame will easily segue into film fame and plenty of performers who've achieved high profiles in television drama or comedy embark on film careers only to find they end up taking leads or supporting roles in mediocre genre productions, or fail altogether to establish themselves in film and so return to television. As Clooney's character Danny Ocean remarks in a playful piece of self-reflection from *Ocean's Eleven* (2001), 'It's hard to do isn't it, crossing over, from television to film?'

It is impossible to definitively explain why some television actors just don't 'make it' in film. Given how star discourse so frequently celebrates the exceptionality of the individual, easy explanations might attribute success or failure to an actor's singular talent alone. What this view ignores is how wider technological, social, economic, industrial and institutional factors distinguish between television and film as performance media. Since its inception, television has generally been conceived of as a domestic medium embedded in the regularized routines of everyday life. In comparison, historical associations with the ceremonial out-of-home public space of the cinema have meant that the feature film has represented spectacular specialness. Consequently, if television is 'ordinary', film appears extraordinary (Langer 1981). Harsh distinctions between these media may have been disrupted by television presentation of movies, the popularization of home video, and use of mobile technologies to view film or television anytime and anywhere. Still, deeply embedded hierarchical beliefs remain about the aesthetic and cultural 'superiority' of film over the 'inferiority' of television. Film's 'big screen' overshadows television's 'small screen'. Escalating investment in high-quality long-form television drama has narrowed the economic and aesthetic gap but is uncharacteristic of television production more generally, for the relatively modest investments made in producing sitcoms or reality formats continue to make television appear like the 'cheap' medium.

Perhaps the most obvious sign of these enduring beliefs is the eager migration of creative talent – directors, writers, actors – from television to film. For many actors, regular work in a television series will likely offer greater employment and financial stability than theatre or film. For an elite of performers, however, film still pays better than even the best television work, and although most performers in either medium don't enjoy those riches, the rewards of appearing in film continue to remain a higher aspiration for the acting community. When actors attempt to move from television to film, they must confront the challenge of how to successfully negotiate the transition between two modes of fame. P. David Marshall (1997: 119) argues that while 'the film celebrity plays with aura through the construction of distance, the television celebrity is configured around conceptions of familiarity'. Moving from television to film, an actor attempts to leave a realm of quotidian fame located in the sphere of the domestic, the familial and the routine, for a context in which fame is constructed through the exceptional, the extraordinary and the spectacular. Such can be the difficulty of making this change that one actor's story has become something of a cautionary tale in modern television folklore. After achieving high-profile visibility in television cop series *NYPD Blue* (1993–2005), David Caruso left during the second season after a dispute over pay. On the back of *NYPD Blue*, Caruso was 'hot' and immediately picked up lead feature film roles, including *Kiss of Death* (1995) and *Jade* (1995). When these failed commercially, Caruso had to return to working in television crime drama, occasionally interspersed with film assignments. Accordingly, Caruso's career crash still serves as an apocryphal warning of the hubristic perils of presuming television fame can be swiftly parlayed into film stardom.

Focusing on the five years from 1994 to 1999 when Clooney was working on *ER* while taking lead feature-film roles, this chapter examines the tensions and conflicts at work in Clooney's passage between differing modes of screen-acting fame. Rather than a smooth and seamless transition, it shows how Clooney's movement between media confronted resistances and frictions. Emphasis is placed particularly on how film reviewers in the US press responded to and evaluated Clooney's film work during this period. In their role as discriminatory gatekeepers, reviewers have the power to confer legitimacy on performers, not only assessing if an actor gives a good or a bad performance but also determining whether s/he should be recognized and classified as a credible film performer. Critical responses to Clooney's early film leads provide points from which to appreciate how his move from television to film was in part mediated and regulated through the critical institution of press reporting. These concerns are focused in case studies exploring the production and reception of Clooney's appearances in *Batman & Robin* (1997) and *Out of Sight* (1998), films that represented respectively the rejection and acceptance of Clooney's status as a credible film lead. By problematizing the inevitability or predictability of Clooney's achievement of star status, the chapter highlights how moving between television and film stands as both opportunity and risk in the production of post-studio Hollywood stardom.

Television fame, *ER* and the emergence of the Clooney brand

In trajectories of modern screen-acting fame, television frequently does not represent a medium in its own right, but rather signifies merely a springboard to other things. As one magazine profile of Clooney noted, 'TV's great promise to an actor has always been to deliver him from TV. Come join our show, it beckons, so soon you can ditch it and make movies. Prime time is acting purgatory, a thespian penitentiary, a celebrity gaol' (Friedman 1998).

Clooney's entry to television came when, as a child, he'd make appearances in commercials and on the Cincinnati talk show hosted by his father, Nick (Brodie 1995: 199). As Clooney's aunt, Rosemary, was a renowned music-recording artist, nepotistic connections meant he did not enter the media and entertainment business from scratch. After deciding to take up a career as a professional actor, Clooney spent 1982 to 1994 mixing television and film work. In television, his on-screen status oscillated from bit parts to supporting characters and leads, all of which failed to bring him any commercial or critical success. Appearances in *Riptide* (1984–6), *Street Hawk* (1985), *Crazy Like a Fox* (1984–6), *Hotel* (1983–8), *Throb* (1986–8), *Hunter* (1984–91), *Jack's Place* (1992–), *Murder, She Wrote* (1984–96), *The Golden Girls* (1985–92) and *The Building* (1993–) saw Clooney taking supporting roles in single episodes of network television series. More stability and continuity was provided with recurring supporting roles for multiple episodes of the sitcoms *E/R* (1984–5) (a medical comedy, not to be confused with *ER*), *The Facts of Life* (1979–88), *Baby Talk* (1991–2) and *Roseanne* (1988–97), and the dramas *Bodies of Evidence* (1992–3) and *Sisters* (1991–6). While many of the series Clooney appeared in were axed after one or two seasons, *Murder, She Wrote*, *The Golden Girls* and *Roseanne* enjoyed long-term popularity on the US networks and sold to overseas markets. As Clooney only appeared in minor roles, however, none of that success could be attributed to his presence. Greater visibility was achieved with leads in pilot episodes for the NBC sitcom *Bennett Brothers* (1987), and CBS's sitcom *Knights of the Kitchen Table* (1990) and crime drama *Rewrite for Murder* (1991), but as these failed to sell to the networks they provided no platform for achieving television fame. Similarly, Clooney played significant supporting roles in NBC's comedy *Combat High* (1986) and disaster drama *Without Warning: Terror in the Towers* (1993), a couple of made-for-TV movies poorly received by reviewers. As one magazine profile once described this phase in Clooney's career, 'he got bad parts on TV shows that were good or good parts on TV shows that were bad' (Junod 2013: 129). Clooney's feature-film career was equally uninspiring. After appearing as an extra in *And They're Off* (1982), Clooney played bit parts in *Grizzly II: The Concert* (1987) and *The Harvest* (1992), larger supporting roles in *Return to Horror High* (1987), *Return of the Killer Tomatoes* (1988) and *The Magic Bubble* (aka *Un-becoming Age*) (1992), and the lead in *Red Surf* (1990). Independently produced and distributed, these films positioned Clooney outside of Hollywood.

ER marked the turning point. Produced by the television division of Steven Spielberg's Amblin Entertainment in conjunction with Warner Bros. Television, for its first five seasons the hospital drama featured Clooney as paediatrician Dr Doug Ross. Before *ER* came along, Clooney had yet to carry the lead for any outright hit, yet Warner Bros. was already cultivating him as television-star material by offering him pilots for six series including the cop drama *Golden Gate*. For that show, Clooney would have been the star headliner, but *ER* placed him in an ensemble cast. Clooney later reasoned that the decision to integrate himself into an ensemble rather than take the lead was because 'up to this point ... my career had not really been known for doing great television .... So I needed some camouflage' (quoted in Brodie 1995: 200). This gamble paid off, with *ER* immediately becoming a primetime hit for the NBC network, and providing a platform for boosting Clooney's film career. By the time he exited *ER*, Clooney had taken leads in a body of films that established him as a leading man working within Hollywood, starting with *From Dusk Till Dawn* (1996) and continuing with *One Fine Day* (1996), *Batman & Robin*, *The Peacemaker* (1997), *Out of Sight* and *Three Kings* (1999).

ER played a key role in defining the Clooney brand for several reasons. First, as a series with strategic value for primetime scheduling, *ER* positioned Clooney as a leading attraction in hit television. Since the early 1980s, NBC had worked at dominating Thursday- night ratings, branding blocks of primetime programming as 'America's Best Night of Television on Television' and collectively labelling Thursday-night comedies 'Must See TV'. Broadcast at 10.00 pm on Thursdays for the entirety of its fifteen-year run, *ER* was exactly placed to occupy the same slot in the schedules and continue NBC's tradition of 'quality drama' previously represented by *Hill Street Blues* (1981–7) and *L.A. Law* (1986–94) (Lowry 1994: 31). Talking about the decision to make *ER* the network's flagship show for the 1994 season, Warren Littlefield, president of NBC's entertainment division, said 'The ultimate answer for what NBC felt about *ER* is in the placement ... We have a tradition in that slot that's nearly sacred ... and we don't take that pact lightly' (quoted in Brodie 1995: 200). After a feature-length pilot aired on Monday 19 September 1994, the first season of *ER* commenced three nights later, timed directly to compete against CBS's own hospital drama *Chicago Hope* (1994–2000), debuting on the same date. *ER* was therefore intentionally positioned as 'appointment TV' designed to capture strong ratings. As *ER* asserted its hold on Thursday nights during the first season, rival networks rescheduled their programming to avoid the competition (Brodie 1995: 198). Over the seasons in which Clooney appeared, *ER* annually ranked first or second among primetime US network programming, which at the time the show aired pulled in approximately a one-third share of all US television sets in use (Table 1.1).

Secondly, Clooney had previously played recurrent but supporting roles in popular shows, or leads in failures, but with *ER* he became a long-term recurrent lead in hit television. As a member of a core ensemble cast, however, he had no outright star

Table 1.1 Annual Ratings *ER* (1994–99) [a]

	Season	Ranking [b]	Rating [c]	Share [d]
5th	24 Sept. 1998–20 May 1999	1	17.8	29
4th	25 Sept. 1997–14 May 1998	2	20.7	34
3rd	26 Sept. 1996–15 May 1997	1	21.2	35
2nd	21 Sept. 1995–16 May 1996	1	22.0	36
1st	19 Sept. 1994–18 May 1995	2	20.0	33

Sources: Quigley (1996: 17A; 1997: 20A; 1998: 23A; 1999: 20; and 2000: 24

Notes

[a]Data limited to the five seasons Clooney appeared in.
[b]Position among top primetime programmes in the season.
[c]Percentage of all television households.
[d]Percentage of television sets in use tuned to the show.

status. The emergency room at Chicago's County General Hospital brought together multiple storylines, some played out in a single episode, others continued across multiple episodes. Television drama series may commonly organize episodes with two main narratives supplemented by minor storylines, but with any episode of *ER* a dozen or more storylines ran without any taking precedence. Frequently stories were set up but then left without offering an eventual closure. This decentred narrative organization was complemented by a highly kinetic visual style of mobile camerawork and fast editing, moving rapidly between scenes and spaces to convey the frenetic collective efforts of the hospital staff. Structure and style therefore coalesced to ensure no singular protagonist anchored the drama; instead narrative agency was dispersed among a core ensemble of recurring characters. In the first five seasons, the core ensemble comprised Clooney, Anthony Edwards, Noah Wyle, Julianna Margulies, and Eriq La Salle (Figure 1.1). For parts of those seasons, Sherry Stringfield, Gloria Reuben, Laura Innes, Maria Bello and Alex Kingston also featured in the core cast. Second billed in the opening 'Starring' credits, Clooney's name held the status of lead-in-an-ensemble-of-leads. Similar cast hierarchies are commonplace in television sitcom and drama, including Clooney's own previous work. What is significant, however, is how this pattern carried over into Clooney's film career. Clooney has certainly occupied the status of singular lead protagonist for films including *Solaris* (2002), *Michael Clayton* (2007), *Up in the Air* (2009), *The American* (2010) and *The Descendants* (2011). At the same time, he's repeatedly belonged to core ensembles for *The Perfect Storm* (2000), the *Ocean's* trilogy (2001, 2004, 2007), *Syriana* (2005), *Burn After Reading* (2008) and *The Monuments Men* (2014). Much of Clooney's film stardom has therefore been modelled on narrative structures and on-screen hierarchies more usually found in television drama.

Thirdly, *ER* also contributed to setting Clooney's on-screen identity within certain generic parameters. With its catalogue

Figure 1.1 Star ensemble. The core cast of *ER* (clockwise from top left, Clooney, Julianna Margulies, Noah Wyle, Gloria Reuben, Anthony Edwards, Laura Innes and Eriq La Salle) ('ER' © Warner Bros. Television & The National Broadcasting Company (NBC) 1994–2009. All rights reserved).

of fatalities, births, gunshot wounds, multi-vehicle accident injuries, suicides, drug overdoses and emotional traumas, *ER* placed Clooney in a soap opera narrative world very strongly inclined towards the melodramatic and sentimental. Gravity was periodically punctured by moments of levity as staff engaged in play, dancing, singing, pranking and joking. As Dr Ross, Clooney occupied both strands of this tonal divide. Week by week he'd routinely battle to save lives. Specializing in the treatment of children, Ross/Clooney not only worked to fix the corporeal sufferings of the young but also protected and defended their emotional needs, admonishing child-abusing parents or providing the care and attention they maybe missed at home. Ross/Clooney became the 'children's champion'.[1] This professional attentiveness was given explanation by a vaguely Oedipal motivation arising from battling personal demons surrounding a conflictual relationship with his estranged father. He emerged an ordinary hero, admired for his everyday caring rather than any grand victorious actions. Amid all the tears and traumas, at the same time he found moments to laugh. Ross/Clooney didn't engage in overtly comedic incidents; rather his serious commitment to the wellbeing of the young was balanced with a general lightness of manner, contributing to the overall camaraderie among the ER staff, and occasionally taking time out to play basketball with colleagues. Melodrama also linked to associations with screen romance. Ross/Clooney was configured as a desirable on-screen presence through his handsome looks, charming self-deprecating manner, and emotional fragility. Ross's troubled love for Nurse Carol Hathaway (played by Margulies) was established in the pilot episode, where it was suggested Hathaway has taken an overdose after breaking up with Ross. This incident immediately set in place Ross's core emotional problem – his superficial and frequently destructive relationships with women, a quality inherited from his father. Struggling to shake off the paternal legacy, it is clear Ross will only find happiness and fulfilment if he can truly learn to love. Deep down, the serial womanizer is in his heart a committed romantic. For much of the time Clooney spent on the show, the relationship with Hathaway only simmered, but was renewed in season four before his departure part way through season five. With few exceptions (e.g. *The Perfect Storm* or *The American*), this mixing of the dramatic (and occasionally the romantic) with the light has set the tonal parameters of Clooney's on-screen identity. Furthermore, this role as conscientious carer for the vulnerable was not only replayed in later roles (e.g. *Three Kings*) but also through his humanitarian work (see Chapter 4).

Finally, while on-screen Clooney remained integrated into the core ensemble, as the popularity of *ER* built, intense off-screen press interest hierarchically differentiated him from the rest of the cast. All the cast individually received media coverage but in Clooney's case the scale progressively distinguished him from his on-screen colleagues. This process started early on. As part of advance publicity, on the Friday before the pilot aired, Clooney was selected by NBC to represent *ER* on Jay Leno's *The Tonight Show* (Brodie 1995: 196). Two early examples indicate how press coverage for *ER* formed a tension between ensemble-belonging and star distinction. Halfway through the first season, an early on-set report for *People* magazine from January 1995 equitably offered anecdotes for each of the core cast members. That Clooney was introduced to readers as 'the Kentucky-born veteran of eight TV shows' may indicate that despite the visibility achieved with his previous television work, there remained a presumption that readers still needed to be introduced to him (Cunneff and Feldon-Mitchell 1995: 95). At the same time, he was already singled out as an object of attention and desire. Just a month after the *People* article, an edition of *TV Guide* carried an image of Clooney as Ross on the front with the main cover line 'Hot Doc!' Opening with the question 'Just how hot is George Clooney these days?', the accompanying story – 'Swooning Over Clooney' – answered by reproducing adoring quotes from online postings made by female fans (Schwed 1995: 13). Clooney was expressly presented as a star for female audiences, with his desirability asserted in magazine profiles with titles like 'Heartthrob Hotel' (Conant 1996) and 'Gorgeous George' (Pearlman 1997), reaching its peak in 1997 with *People* magazine conferring the title 'Sexiest Man Alive' (Sanz 1997).

Once Clooney's film work began to take off, media interest in him only increased, so that over time, sustained press coverage had the cumulative effect of lifting Clooney out of the *ER* ensemble. 'True, *ER* is an ensemble series that benefits from a brilliant troupe of players,' *TV Guide* acknowledged, '[b]ut at this particular moment, it is Clooney's turn to get the breakthrough attention' (Schwed 1995: 13). This partially reflected back onto Ross/Clooney's on-screen status, with the series occasionally breaking from its normal narrative pattern to go with episodes almost entirely focused on Ross. In 'Hell and High Water,' the seventh episode of season two, Ross is contemplating taking a job at a private practice when circumstances lead to him saving a boy trapped in a flooded storm drain, a moment of self-realization that renews his vocational dedication to public healthcare. Although not the only story that week, the rescue took precedence, and in what might be read as a reflexive comment on the differentiation of Clooney from the ensemble, Ross's heroism leads to him becoming the focus of frenzied media attention. Two years later, in 'Fathers and Sons', the seventh episode of season four, Edwards's character Mark Greene accompanies Ross as he travels to Barstow following the death of his father. Removing Greene and Ross from Chicago distanced the pair from the core cast, with the episode reserving time for a mini road movie in which both characters go on personal journeys as they reflect on paternal relations. During Clooney's five seasons on *ER*, Edwards was also granted a 'solo' episode, but it was Clooney who was positioned on- and off-screen as the principal attraction. As one commentator noted, Clooney had become 'the man who anchors the show that anchors the night that anchors the network and anchors television' (Friedman 1998).

When Clooney decided to leave the series, he along with executive producer John Wells, Warner Bros. and NBC, all agreed the departure should come mid-season, giving the drama time to build up momentum prior to the exit and create new storylines afterwards. *People* called Clooney's departure the 'End of an *ER*-A' (Gilatto 1999). Despite the star value he'd acquired over the five years, when Clooney left *ER* he was still receiving the $42,000 per episode agreed in his original contract, compared to the $360,000 per episode commanded by Edwards and $300,000 by Wyle (Fleming 1998a). *ER* undoubtedly gave Clooney his 'break', elevating him from jobbing television and film actor to TV star, but as television fame offers no guarantees of film fame, questions persisted over whether he'd achieve similar popularity in film. Acknowledging the perils of jumping from television to film, and aware of his own uninspiring record in film, when the first *ER* season was still airing Clooney wisely reflected:

You don't want to come out and say 'Okay, now give me a million bucks and let me carry a film' the first time out after a hit television series ... Because then you're Richard Grieco, and it's gone pretty quickly.[2] The secret to surviving is not to go for the whole right at once. You want to come out and do a good third or fourth lead.

(quoted in Brodie 1995: 198)

Playing Dr Ross, Clooney achieved the familiarization effect of television fame, appearing in living rooms regularly on Thursday nights for over 100 episodes across five seasons aired over four and a half years. With actors in long-running television dramas, Marshall (1997: 128) argues one outcome of the familiarization process is that the regular audience's 'full and intimate sense of knowledge of the individual soap opera character ... impedes the possibility of an actor in a soap opera becoming known beyond his or her role'. Rather than a step up, the familiarity achieved by television fame may actually become a burden, presenting an obstacle to film stardom. *ER* was therefore good for Clooney but he still had to prove himself as a credible leading man in film.

Struggling for filmic legitimization

With his early film work, Clooney operated in the independent production and distribution sector, but on the back of the high-profile visibility he achieved through *ER*, he quickly received a flurry of offers from divisions of the Hollywood majors. As the first season of *ER* neared its end, in mid-April 1995 Clooney was recruited to the cast of *From Dusk Till Dawn*, produced by the Disney subsidiary Miramax. Director Quentin Tarantino had written the film some years before and had directed Clooney in *ER*'s twenty-fourth episode, 'Motherhood'. For *From Dusk Till Dawn*, however, he took a break from directing to act opposite Clooney as one half of the gun-toting brothers Richard and Seth Gecko. Miramax described the film as Clooney's 'first feature-length starring role' (quoted in Cox 1995: 3), although in the opening credits Clooney was second billed after Harvey Keitel. Shortly after the second season of *ER* commenced, in October 1995 industry rumour was linking Clooney's name to multiple feature projects, including *The M Word* for Warner Bros., *Blue Streak* and *Desperate Measures* for TriStar, *The Bookworm* for Fox and *The Saint* for Paramount (Fleming 1995a). Clooney never committed to these projects but did agree a $3 million deal to appear as the crime-fighting lead in *The Green Hornet*, a new franchise from Universal based on the 1930s radio show (Busch 1995). These plans had to be aborted, however, when in December 1995 Steven Spielberg poached Clooney for the lead in action drama *The Peacemaker*. The film was the first production from the new studio DreamWorks SKG, a venture launched by Spielberg in collaboration with former Disney executive Jeffrey Katzenberg and music mogul David Geffen. As Spielberg's Amblin company produced *ER*, there was an established link between the director and Clooney. Spielberg exercised his influence to extract Clooney from the *Green Hornet* deal by agreeing he'd direct a *Jurassic Park* (1993) sequel for Universal (Fleming 1995b). A month after signing for *The Peacemaker*, however, Clooney accepted $3 million for *One Fine Day*, a romantic comedy from Fox 2000 pairing him with Michelle Pfeiffer, and then in February 1996 he signed to *Batman & Robin* as part of a $25 million three-picture deal with Warner Bros., rumoured to include an option for him to appear in a Batman sequel (Busch and Dawtry 1996: 1).

Woven between working on seasons of *ER*, these films established Clooney as a leading male in film although the lack of consistency in the roles or genres he appeared in prevented him from stabilizing a clear star brand in film. A season and a half of *ER* had passed by 19 January 1996 when *From Dusk Till Dawn* received its North American release. Any familiar image of Clooney as the saviour of lives, protector of children and wooer of women was immediately cast aside with the film's opening sequence, where Seth engages in violent gun play and kills a liquor store clerk by setting fire to him. Clooney had only spent one season as the caring but tortured Dr Ross when he worked on *From Dusk Till Dawn*. Still, when Seth torches the clerk, metaphorically the moment signals an aggressive symbolic parting of Clooney's television and film careers. *From Dusk Till Dawn* was a peculiar generic hybrid, starting as a gun crime road movie before radically changing course for a second half of splatter horror when the Gecko brothers end up in a bar populated by vampires. In many ways this generic inconsistency encapsulated the instability characterizing this phase of Clooney's film career. After the bloody violence of *From Dusk Till Dawn*, the romcom sweetness of *One Fine Day*, released on 20 December 1996 – mid-way through season three of *ER* – fit more easily with preconceptions spilling over from Clooney's television fame. *Batman & Robin*, however, took Clooney off in new directions, inserting him into a campy take on a well-run comic book franchise before *The Peacemaker* went in a further direction with an action thriller.

Bouncing between divergent generic forms, Clooney's film career lacked focus and definition. This seemed to have little effect, though, on critical perceptions of Clooney's credibility as a film actor. Doubt was expressed that '*From Dusk Till Dawn* gives no reason to assume that George Clooney, playing the least compelling criminal in the Tarantino oeuvre, will have an easier passage from TV to movie stardom than David Caruso' (Hoberman 1996). Otherwise, however, critical opinion readily hailed Clooney as an emergent star.

Mr Clooney turns out to be an impressive presence on the big screen, a star presence and yet a likeable actor free of stylistic tics or encumbering ego.

(Morgenstern 1996)

a good movie star turn: he seizes the screen and melts it.

(Corliss 1996)

As to Clooney, it's clear he has more than enough charm and looks to ricochet smoothly into leading parts. And unlike, say, David Caruso, he understands the value of a choice TV gig ... He also has brains – he's launched his movie career while tucked in the midst of a first-rate if excessively hip ensemble distinguished by Keitel and [Juliette] Lewis.

(Dargis 1996)

[the film] transforms Clooney into a fully-fledged movie star.

(Charity 1996)

As he hops from the ER to the abattoir, George Clooney is the best reason to submit yourself to 'From Dusk Till Dawn'.

(Hunter 1996: 12)

demand[ing] attention by a wider audience is George Clooney's instant emergence as a full-fledged movie star.

(McCarthy 1996a: 98)

Even those not tuned into [Robert] Rodriguez and Tarantino's gross-out trip might want to check this out for Clooney's star-making breakthrough.

(McCarthy 1996a: 100)

Similarly, *One Fine Day* received mixed notices from reviewers but generally opinion positively judged Clooney's contribution to the film.

With appealing star performances from Michelle Pfeiffer and George Clooney, this charmer should attract very fine days at the boxoffice.

(Byrge 1996: 9)

Clooney ... proves he's a leading man. And I do mean leading man, not an overgrown brat or one more tremulous incarnation of vulnerable-boy James Dean. In this age of eternally teenage suburban superstars and endless gender confusion, he acts as if he enjoys being a guy of the world.

(Sragow 1996)

[*One Fine Day*] marks the emergence of George Clooney as a major romantic star.

The confident Clooney, 'ER's' hospital heart-throb, didn't play to his strength when he debuted in the ultra-violent 'From Dusk Till Dawn,' but it's different here. With his thick eyebrows and perpetual 5 o'clock shadow, Clooney possesses considerable roguish charm and handles himself with practiced aplomb.

(Turan 1996: F1)

Clooney, in his second post-'E.R.' stardom feature, makes it all look easy, effortlessly conveying both the capable, tenacious, professional side of his character and the romantic softy inside .... [He] shows a light touch that offers further evidence of considerable range and ability to dominate on the bigscreen.

(McCarthy 1996b)

delivery of his opening line, 'This is why Superman works alone', Clooney's distinctive voice might enhance identification of the actor (see Chapter 2) but then promptly the film is taken away from him again with a protracted action sequence in which Batman and Robin do battle with Mr Freeze. A terse Batman is only seen at a distance. Physically, this could be anyone, and given the high-cost risks required to protect leading talent from harm, it could be reasonably presumed that at many points during the sequence a stuntman is carrying the role.

Shrouded in anonymity, Clooney's entrance and opening scenes reflect his overall status in the film. When out of the bat suit, Clooney is entirely visible as Bruce Wayne, but as Wayne only gets fourteen short scenes in the whole two hours, he holds less screen time than Batman or the villains. Even during those scenes, the script cedes the narrative to other actors, so that when he is visible as Wayne, Clooney appears as a brief or peripheral figure. *Batman & Robin* mixes action and comedy with elements of pantomime and slapstick, but as a superhero tale the focus would conventionally always be on the capacity to act. Yet Clooney as Wayne or Batman exercises no catalytic authority; apart from the final inevitable vanquishing of Freeze, Batman/Clooney remains a reactive force, a figure more done to than doing. *Batman & Robin* is a superhero movie that doesn't even grant the hero the space to be heroic.

Some reviewers judged Clooney's incarnation of Batman in positive terms:

'Batman & Robin' are a dynamic duo in this latest Warner Bros.' franchise, thanks chiefly to the charismatic performance of George Clooney as the leather-suited hero … Imbuing his character with a subtler charm than past performances have rendered, Clooney is a terrific Gotham-ite.

(Byrge 1997a: 8 and 40)

As the third Batman/Bruce Wayne in four movies, George Clooney is soulful and ironic, finding the humor in his character's ability to take huge surprises in his stride.

(Bernstein 1997)

For other reviewers, however, the significance of the character and the franchise overwhelmingly exceeded that of the actor.

Physically, Clooney is unquestionably the most ideal Batman to date, but none of the series' screenwriters has ever gotten a handle on how to make the character as interesting as those around him, and Clooney is unable to compensate for that lack of dimension. It is difficult to think of another superhero series in which it would matter so little who plays the part, and it is indicative of the ongoing flaw in the Batman franchise that the changes in leading men have so little impact on the films' popularity or effectiveness.

(McCarthy 1997a: 37)

These challenges face any actor who plays Batman, but still Clooney was judged to fall short of what previous actors had achieved in the role:

In the hands of George Clooney, who lacks the dark irony of a Michael Keaton or twisted dramatics of a Val Kilmer, the Caped Crusader is but a cipher in rubber.

(Lambert 1997)

Of all modern Batmans, George Clooney bears the closest physical resemblance to the comic-book hero, but there isn't much to say about his performance because there isn't much performance to discuss.

(Morgenstern 1997)

Some expressed a belief that Clooney would achieve stardom but regarded *Batman & Robin* as stalling or hampering that progress:

Clooney, charming in 'One Fine Day,' neither hinders nor advances his chances at movie stardom here.

(Turan 1997b)

You leave Batman & Robin convinced that Clooney will indeed be a star, but weeping with frustration that he chose to do so with this hectic, gibbering film – which is enough to send any man back into the arms of Nurse Hathaway.

(Shone 1997: 5)

Given the history of failures in translating television fame into film fame, reviewers doubted whether Clooney would escape the small screen: 'Even Clooney's bedroom smile makes no impact; if anything, I suspect an imminent case of Caruso syndrome, which causes actors to quit well-written TV shows in favour of movies that are barely written at all' (Lane 1997a: 77).

In *Batman & Robin* Clooney occupied a contradictory position, 'starring' as an anonymous presence. After the film's relatively poor commercial performance, Warner not only chose not to take up the sequel option in Clooney's contract but also halted the whole film series until its 'reboot' with *Batman Begins* (2005). Despite the film's high-profile market visibility, *Batman & Robin* did not provide a platform for stardom. Rather, Warner's Batman series of the 1980s and 1990s pioneered the growth of superhero franchises that by the start of the following century displaced star driven vehicles from the forefront of box office popularity. With *Batman & Robin*, Clooney's submersion in a major cross-media franchise at least partially augered the decline of Hollywood star power witnessed in the next decade (see Chapter 3 and the Conclusion).

Out of Sight and the defining of the Clooney brand

Although Clooney completed work on *The Peacemaker* before
starting *Batman & Robin*, the former was released three months
after the latter. Commencing its North American theatrical run
on 26 September 1997, *The Peacemaker* opened the day after the
fourth series of *ER* started. Launched at this point in the release
calendar, *The Peacemaker* fell outside the main summer season
but the distributor still gave the film event movie status, opening
domestically across 2,362 screens. As DreamWorks' first feature
production a lot rested on *The Peacemaker*, but given the scale of
release, the total worldwide gross of $110 million ($41.3 million
domestic, $69.2 million international) disappointed expectations.
Among reviewers Clooney's performance drew mixed opinions.
Some were lukewarm in their judgments:

George Clooney looks ominously lightweight; I am as vulnerable to his
blowtorch smile as anyone else, but did he really have to keep it turned up
full when the nuke was seven seconds away from ground zero? Don't tell
George, but cool can back into dumb.

(Lane 1997b)

Clooney, in a clunky clunky way, devoid of lightning but with a touch of
thunder, fills the space in the story that he is meant to occupy ...

(Kauffmann 1997)

There are hints at the outset that Clooney's bad-boy officer is meant to be a
charming lady killer and professional scoundrel, but the attempts to give him
Bond-like bon mots are only halfhearted, and there is simply no time amidst
the chases and explosions to develop anything resembling a relationship,
much less a romance.

(McCarthy 1997b: 18)

Others believed, however, that Clooney comfortably fitted his role and welcomed his move into the action genre:

Clooney, with his salt-and-pepper flair and seat-of-his-pants daring, is a believable and wonderfully appealing action hero ...

Although his constant head tilting has become somewhat of a distraction, Clooney's suave edginess brings a welcome verve to a genre in need of tone rather than bulk.

(Byrge 1997b: 14)

Both [Nicole] Kidman and Clooney give dependable, movie-star performances in these James Bond-ish roles ... And though Clooney is the same dark-eyed smiling rogue he's played in just about all his feature roles, it's a characterization that is effective.

(Turan 1997a: F16)

[Clooney is] naturally well cast as a charming roué.

(Maslin 1997)

After the calamity of *Batman & Robin*, *The Peacemaker* at least preserved some belief among critical gatekeepers that Clooney could still be a credible leading man in a piece of popular cinema.

A few days after *The Peacemaker* opened, on 1 October 1997 Clooney commenced work on the comedy crime drama *Out of Sight*. Adapted from the Elmore Leonard novel of the same name, *Out of Sight* was developed by Jersey Films, the company of actor-producer-director Danny DeVito and producers Michael Shamberg and Stacey Sher. Clooney was contracted to the project in February 1997 for a fee of $10 million, but as he was still to work through the three-picture deal agreed when signing for *Batman & Robin*, Warner Bros. had to give him clearance to work on the Universal production (Dunkley 1997; Fleming 1997). Steven Soderbergh was hired to direct a month later, and in May, Jennifer

Lopez joined the cast (Busch 1997a and 1997b). Made for $45 million and grossing only $77.7 million worldwide, *Out of Sight* once again gave no evidence that Clooney could be a compelling commercial attraction. In retrospect, however, *Out of Sight* appears a star-defining film, stabilizing the inconsistencies of Clooney's previous roles by bringing together many of the features and qualities that subsequently marked his on-screen brand and, most importantly, winning unanimous acceptance among reviewers of his star credibility.

Clooney's previous four films had pulled him in many directions across horror, romcom, superhero camp, and action. Combining crime with comedy and romance, *Out of Sight* set out a range of generic credentials that would reappear at various points across Clooney's subsequent career. *Out of Sight* therefore became crucial to defining the Clooney brand. His character, the career bank robber Jack Foley, assisted by his sidekick Buddy (Ving Rhames), breaks out of Glades Correctional Institution. When US Marshall Karen Sisco (Lopez) attempts to stop them, they bundle her into the trunk of a car, where she is joined by Foley. This chance meeting establishes the film's double chase narrative. In part the film is a crime-comedy with Sisco/Lopez pursuing Foley/Clooney from Miami to Detroit as he aims to steal a cache of uncut diamonds from corrupt businessman Richard Ripley (Albert Brooks), known to Foley after the two served time together in Lompoc Federal Penitentiary. At the same time the mutual attraction between Foley/Clooney and Sisco/Lopez creates a romance narrative in which Sisco undertakes a secondary pursuit of her man. It is this mix of generic credentials that makes *Out of Sight* so important to the definition of the Clooney brand. Links between crime and comedy reappeared with Clooney's next lead film role, Archie Gates in the Gulf War adventure *Three Kings*, followed by the *Ocean's* trilogy and *Welcome to Collinwood* (2002). All were, in their different ways, heist capers. Comedy more generally also continued to characterize Clooney's output. Working with the director-producer-writer duo Joel and Ethan Coen, Clooney made the idiosyncratic comedies *O Brother, Where Art Thou?* (2000) (see Chapter 2), *Intolerable Cruelty* (2003), *Burn After Reading* (2008) and *Hail, Caesar!* (2016). When Clooney moved onto directing (see Chapter 3), comedy remained a component of his films, with the espionage caper *Confessions of a Dangerous Mind* (2002), screwball comedy *Leatherheads* (2008) and light-hearted war drama *The Monuments Men* (2014). After the relationship between Ross and Hathaway in *ER*, and the romcom conventions of *One Fine Day*, romance sporadically reappeared across Clooney's output. In *Ocean's Eleven*, the only reason Danny Ocean/Clooney is trying to rob the casino vault is to get back at the man who stole his wife. Love deceives Ryan Bingham/Clooney in *Up in the Air* (2009), and for *Intolerable Cruelty* and *Leatherheads*, the conventions of screwball ensure the couple are together at the end. Comedy and romance are therefore integral to the Clooney brand, although his output has remained too diverse for him to be solely labelled either a comedic or a romantic star.

Leonard once remarked of the characters in his novels 'most of those guys are dumb, so there's humor waiting to pop up … I don't write comedy – everyone in my books is very serious – but the humor is there' (quoted in Baker 2013). Clooney's role fits effectively into Leonard's world for Foley is a straight guy mixed up with a humorous ensemble of distinctive multi-ethnic characters played by Rhames, Don Cheadle, Luis Guzmán, Steve Zahn and Brooks. In *Out of Sight* the intersection of comedy with romance is not only a product of generic conventions but also of performance. Two scenes demonstrate this enactment of the Clooney brand. From the opening scene, the mix of the comedic and the straight is immediately evident in *Out of Sight*. Foley is established as a cool and skilful bank robber but also a bit dumb. At the opening Foley/Clooney emerges from an office building and in a fit of rage rips off his tie: only much later is it explained he is upset by the lowly security guard job he's just been offered by his former prison acquaintance Ripley/Brooks. Acting on impulse Foley/Clooney crosses the street to the Sun Trust Bank where he successfully persuades a teller, Loretta Randall (Donna Frenzel), to hand over a large quantity of cash. The scene gives Fo quiet and cool authority, for as the crime is entirely unpremeditate rather than resorting to violence or weapons, Foley/Clooney wins Randall/Frenzel's compliance through improvisational skill. He te her that if she doesn't hand over the money, the bank's assistant manager, seen at a desk across the lobby, will be killed by the person sitting opposite him, a man who Foley claims is his accomplice. In fact, that man has no connection with Foley but is just an innocent customer there to take out a loan. While the story is threatening, Foley/Clooney keeps quiet control, expressing no anger, keeping physically still, speaking in a low, subdued tone, and looking away from Randall/Frenzel (Figure 1.4). In other words, he plays cool. Foley's experience and criminal wisdom is evident, for when Randall retrieves the money from the cash drawer, he calmly instructs her he wants '[n]othing with bank straps or rubber bands. I don't want dye packs. I don't want bait money'. While extorting money, Foley/Clooney gives the exchange the semblance of a chat-up situation, instantly addressing the teller by her first name and fixing her with the same charming smile repeatedly seen in *ER* (Figure 1.5). Responding to her nervousness, he asks if it's the first time she's been robbed, and as she gathers the money, offers caring encouragement, reassuring her 'You're doing great. Just smile so you don't look like you're being held up', before flirtatiously commenting, 'You got a very pretty smile'. Pocketing the money, he then walks casually away, even taking time to interrupt the loan transaction taking place in the lobby to ask the totally bemused customer 'Hey – she's cute, isn't she?' Foley/Clooney is therefore in absolute control. For him, bank robbery is effortless, graceful, even charming. But then this authority is systematically dismantled. After leaving the bank, Foley/Clooney crosses the car park to get into a small and rather tatty Honda Civic. His getaway is thwarted, however, when the vehicle won't start. Now he loses his cool, becoming agitated, swearing and frantically

Figures 1.4–1.6 From debonair charmer to frustrated fool. Foley/Clooney gets the money but bungles the getaway in *Out of Sight* ('Out of Sight' directed by Steven Soderbergh © Universal Studios 1998. All rights reserved).

pumping the gas pedal, at which point he is arrested by two armed guards. The moment is comic, not only because Foley is foiled in entirely ridiculous circumstances, but his desperate and panicked manners are so at odds with the contained charm and quiet stillness previously performed (Figure 1.6). Contrasting the straight and the comedic, Clooney's performance illustrates how Foley is at once a skilful criminal and a fool.

For the purposes of the romance narrative, Clooney must adopt a different mode of performance. Instead of the fool, Clooney plays the seductive lover. This impulse reaches its apotheosis when Foley/Clooney meets Sisco/Lopez in the bar at the top of a Detroit hotel she is staying in. Visual style, script, performance, music and editing all work together to give the scene its romantic and sexual charge. Although shot on a soundstage, production designer Gary Frutkoff and cinematographer Elliot Davis gave the scene a magical *mise en scène*, with the two actors sitting beside a window, outside which snow appears to gently fall across the flickering lights of the night-time city skyline. The script structures the scene so that Foley fulfils Sisco's desires. Sisco/Lopez is sitting alone in the bar when she is approached by two admen who sequentially try to pull her. She politely gives them the brush-off, but when Foley/Clooney appears, she immediately accepts his offer of a drink and invites him to 'sit down'. If it were not already apparent by this point in the narrative, the moment confirms that in Sisco/Lopez's eyes, he's the only one. Although they know one another, rather than meeting as Jack and Karen, the two indulge in role-playing, assuming the names 'Gary' and 'Celeste' to perform a scene of two strangers meeting for the first time (Figure 1.7). Foley/Clooney quickly discards the pretence and enters into a mini speech about the need to grasp the opportunity when instant attraction is experienced in chance encounters. With his stillness, deep vocal tones, fixed eye contact and slight smile, Clooney adopts a manner of performance appropriate to the intimacy of the scene (Figure 1.8). If at other points in the film Foley/Clooney acts like an

Figures 1.7–1.9 Desires fulfilled. Foley/Clooney and Sisco/Lopez play out their mutual attraction in *Out of Sight* ('Out of Sight' directed by Steven Soderbergh © Universal Studios 1998. All rights reserved).

idiot, here he acts as a seducer. Further adding to the atmosphere is David Holmes's soundtrack, which here quietly introduces trip-hop-inspired non-diegetic music under Foley/Clooney's speech. Editing now disrupts time and space, for as the duologue in the bar and the music continue, the sequence is fractured by the insertion of shots showing the couple in Sisco/Lopez's hotel bedroom (Figure 1.9). In the bedroom they drink, touch, undress and then climb onto the bed together. As these moments are interspersed with the two characters still seen sitting in the bar, the bedroom shots have the status of flash-forwards. They forecast the sex play that will inevitably follow after Sisco/Lopez concludes the bar duologue with 'Let's get out of here'.[3]

In the press, reviewers not only regarded the film as making up for the weaknesses of Clooney's previous films but also as legitimizing his candidature for movie stardom.

The most gratifying thing about the new George Clooney movie, 'Out of Sight,' is that it turns out to be a good George Clooney movie. People were starting to talk. What with 'One Fine Day' and 'The Peacemaker' – not to mention 'Batman and Robin,' which was as much fun as chewing black rubber – it was beginning to look as if Clooney couldn't punch his weight in the big ring.

(Lane 1998)

just as one was beginning to doubt whether Clooney would make the leap from TV star to movie star, he comes up with a performance that mixes charm, edge and rage in beguiling fashion.

(Ansen 1998)

Clooney has never been better. A lot of actors who are handsome when young need to put on some miles before the full flavour emerges. Here Clooney at last looks like a big-screen star.

(Ebert 1998)

Clooney finally comes to his own as the debonair bank robber, a role that combines his good looks and easygoing, laid-back charm.

(Levy 1998: 22)

Out of Sight put into place a set of characteristics that would remain common to the Clooney brand: his positioning as the lead within an ensemble of strongly defined and interesting supporting characters; generic associations with comedy, sometimes combined with crime and/or romance; and matching those generic credentials with a performance style easily juxtaposing suave bodily manners and vocal tones with comedic exaggeration. *Batman & Robin* sold a far greater number of tickets but *Out of Sight* did more to establish Clooney as a plausible star attraction. After the generic incoherence witnessed across *From Dusk Till Dawn, One Fine Day, Batman & Robin* and *The Peacemaker*, the film's contents provided material for embedding a set of meanings around the actor's performed masculine charm and desirability while also starting an association with cool and hip comedy that continued with *Ocean's Eleven* (see Chapter 2).

Conclusion

During the years Clooney worked on *ER*, members of the core ensemble individually acquired nominations and some wins in the acting categories of the Golden Globes, Emmys and Screen Actors Guild (SAG) awards. Four years in a row SAG honoured the collective cast by conferring the award for Outstanding Performance by an Ensemble in a Drama Series. While working on *ER*, or after they left the series, all members of the core ensemble worked in feature films. Apart from Clooney, however, none achieved big screen stardom. Instead, other members of the ensemble largely filled out their CVs with further television work. Historically, as Hollywood has operated within highly circumscribed gender and racial boundaries privileging white masculinity in the definition of stardom, so it was always more likely Clooney would attain star status than any of his female counterparts or La Salle. Still, the *ER* ensemble cast exemplifies the challenges and obstacles confronting actors when leaving hit television for film.

Clooney's eventual film star status should not therefore lead to the presumption that big-screen success was inevitable. From the vantage point of knowing Clooney achieved film stardom, it could be tempting to presume Clooney's success was the outcome of some individually orchestrated plan. This would be to impose an overly rational, mechanistic self-determinist view that ignores the many contingencies that have palpable effects in the production of stardom. By Clooney's own admission, 'If one of those crappy pilots had been picked up, I wouldn't have been available to do *ER*. And if *ER* had been put on Friday night instead of Thursday night, I don't have a film career' (Nashawaty 2005: 48). Rather than individual self-determination or sheer luck, this chapter has viewed Clooney's achievement of film stardom as entailing a process of legitimization negotiated between two arenas of screen fame. *ER* certainly gave Clooney a level of recognition and fame he'd not attained with his previous work but also very visibly associated him with the 'inferior' medium of television. As one article from 2006 reflected, the 'massive and overwhelming success' of his stint as Dr Ross 'may have threatened to permanently embalm Clooney as a TV actor' (Koehler 2006: A2). Television familiarity therefore posed a potential trap. In the late 1990s, when Clooney was still juxtaposing television and film work, he reflected on his early career and acknowledged

the chasm between television and movies is a huge one. I had been working in television for eight years when I had to audition for a two-line bit in *Guarding Tess*, and I was labelled as 'television.' There is a huge difference. Now, a good percentage of movie actors come from television, but the crossover is still tough.

(quoted in Vincent 1998)

Clooney had to achieve credibility as a film performer and *Out of Sight* was decisive in making the break, for while not a huge commercial hit, the film stabilized the meanings of the Clooney brand, creating a vehicle that legitimized him as Hollywood film material.

Notes

1 Thanks to Tamar Jeffers McDonald for suggesting this term.
2 Grieco achieved some popularity as Officer Dennis Booker in the series *21 Jump Street* (1987–91) and *Booker* (1989–90) before struggling to establish a film career and returning to television movies and series.
3 For this device Soderbergh admitted to taking inspiration from Nicholas Roeg's *Don't Look Now* (1973) where a scene of Julie Christie and Donald Sutherland having sex in their hotel bedroom is interspersed with shots of the couple getting dressed to go out.

2 PERFORMING STARDOM: ACTOR/STAR

Like all film actors, Clooney's professional function on-screen is to represent characters using his body and voice, and yet Clooney is not like other actors, for he belongs to that small elite who are actor-stars. Clooney's acting portrays characters who become components in the construction of the narrative worlds he appears in. For example, as Seth Gecko, Clooney fights his way through the bizarre world of *From Dusk Till Dawn* (1996); as Jack Taylor he rushes around New York falling in love during *One Fine Day* (1996); and as Bruce Wayne and Batman he saves Gotham in the superhero fantasy universe of *Batman & Robin* (1997). As each tale is different, Clooney's acting responds to and immerses him in the narrative circumstances of the specific story told. At the same time, Clooney is always the same, for to be a saleable attraction his body and voice must be used in ways that ensure he always remains to some degree visible across the range of roles he plays. Clooney can be Gecko, Taylor or Wayne, but as a star he must always 'play himself'.

Representing different characters while presenting a point of saleable continuity, the movie star is both actor and asset. With the actor-star the body and voice achieve significance by reconciling these dual demands, creating the differences necessary to represent characters inhabiting specific narrative circumstances while at the same time preserving similarities or continuities to present a familiar recognizable element of the overall screen spectacle. Star acting therefore always rests on foundational tensions between difference and similarity, narrative and spectacle, representation and presentation, or story and show (McDonald 2012a; 2012b; and 2013: 183–4). As discussed in the Introduction, film stars and brands are commercial identities; both make distinctive statements in the marketplace by uniting several different products under a singular 'personality'. Producing characters in film always involves more than just acting: script, narrative structure, costume, music and *mise en scène* all contribute to character creation (Dyer 1998: 106–17). A star's branded performance is therefore the creation of multiple inputs, not all of which originate from the star. Where the actor-star does contribute is through the uses of the body and voice to represent character. Acting is that part of film performance specifically attributable to the performer's uses of the body and voice. With the actor-star brand, it is the body and voice that produce the material signs for deploying a distinct performing presence in the film market. Star acting is therefore branded acting.

Focusing on matters of acting and performance, this chapter analyses Clooney as a recognizable branded presence in film. As one commentator notes:

Being George Clooney in a George Clooney movie is a wise place to start if you are George Clooney …. But a rarely understood aspect of movie-star acting is range – and that an actor may appreciate his own range and use it to his advantage is even less understood, which (thus far) has saved us from Clooney as Hamlet or Willy Loman. Instead, we get that stoic brow, those bedroom eyes, the constant hint of a smirk and an effortless cool. He may veer an inch toward gravitas, or an inch toward silliness, but he's always within a narrow range.

[]

'He just plays himself': There's often a wallop of contempt in that charge, lobbed by contemporary audiences at stars with the implication that an actor has grown lazy. But it conveniently ignores that big movie stars intend a degree of repetition … It's also a charge that forgets what makes movies work, and that good actors who happen to be stars have an uncanny understanding of the pros and cons of playing themselves.

The Golden Age of Hollywood's studio system treated contract players as specific brands and assigned them a narrow range, thereby giving audiences what was expected. What it allowed a strong personality to do was create his [sic] own reality, which is what Clooney [does]. It's what Cary Grant did, and Tom Cruise does, and James Cagney did, and Julia Roberts does.

(Borrelli 2010)

As with any actor-star, Clooney's branded acting is a combination of narrative particularity with spectacular sameness. To understand how this is achieved, it is necessary, however, to move past such generalized observations. With acting and performance analysis, the challenge is to look beyond the character creation, i.e. *what* is represented, and to focus instead on *how* that figure is created, in other words to explore the detailed uses of the body and voice in the *enactment* of character. This does not require studying the whole of an act or performance: in fact, it would be a mistake to do so, for this would presume the enactment of star branding is only achieved in the totality of a performance. Instead the branding effects of star performance are the product of small details, the micro actions of the body and voice as these combine with other filmic elements to create character and spectacle. Rather than look at the whole act, the work of analysis is therefore to examine how the actor-star brand is practically enacted in particular scenes (McDonald 2004). Initially this chapter identifies the common bodily and vocal markers that make Clooney a distinctive presence on-screen, before analyses of selected scenes from *O Brother, Where Art Thou?* (2000) and *Ocean's Eleven* (2001) look at specific enactments of the Clooney brand. These films are not only chosen because they appear consecutively in Clooney's career, but because they also show Clooney employing contrasting manners or 'modes' of acting. Looking between the two therefore provides a point from which to observe how uses of the body and voice produce the differences and continuities that mark the branding effects of star acting.

Signs of Clooneyness

Maybe the most immediate way to get into considering the branding of star performance is to ask what are the bodily and vocal markers that signify the Clooneyness of Clooney? Physical resemblance is the obvious starting point. The face alone is enough to brand any star performance: Clooney becomes a branded presence quite simply because the guy playing roles across several films always looks like George Clooney. Taking just the examples discussed in the previous chapter, a square jawline, dark brown eyes and thick eyebrows are among the most noticeable signs of Clooney's presence in *ER* (1994–2009), *From Dusk Till Dawn, One Fine Day, Batman & Robin, The Peacemaker* (1997) and *Out of Sight* (1998). In this period, hair also emerged as an operative marker for Clooney. For much of his television work and early film roles, Clooney sported a full mane of tresses, but to play Seth Gecko in *From Dusk Till Dawn* he radically reshaped his own hair into a 'Caesar' cut – overall short with the fringe brushed forward. 'I just wanted [Gecko] to look like a guy who never had his hair cut ... So I took a razor blade, and cut off all my hair ... But because I was also doing this popular series at the time, the haircut ended up becoming something that I would get known for' (quoted in Potts 2007: 85). Subsequently, the styling certainly changed between roles but Clooney's hair remained within particular limits, with variations on relatively short and usually neat cuts. This groomed 'repertoire' variously served to connote: uniform military regularity in *The Peacemaker, The Thin Red Line* (1998), *Three Kings* (1999), *The Good German* (2006) and *The Monuments Men* (2014); seafaring ruggedness for *The Perfect Storm* (2000); cool smoothness with *Out of Sight* and the *Ocean's* trilogy (2001, 2004 and 2007); professionalized authority in *Michael Clayton* (2007), *Up in the Air* (2009) and *The Ides of March* (2011); and slicked periodicity for *Confessions of a Dangerous Mind* (2002), *Good Night, and Good Luck* (2005), *The Good German, Leatherheads* (2008) and *The Monuments Men*. When returning to a variation on the Caesar cut for *Hail, Caesar!* (2016), this single small detail of appearance mediated between character difference and star similarity: the cut fit with the narrative of fictional 1950s movie star Baird Whitlock playing the part of Roman general Autolochus in a biblical film epic, while at the same time preserving continuity with Clooney's look in *From Dusk Till Dawn* and *ER*.

For an actor so well known for his handsomeness, it is maybe unsurprising that Clooney's looks play such a major part in defining his on-screen visibility. With actor-stars, physical appearances in general, and the face in particular, present the most overt signs of sameness and continuity that anchor branded performance. The face and body become the corporeal substance marking and marketing the performing presence of the actor-star. Yet in playing the differences of multiple characters an actor-star's appearance is never entirely fixed or stable. Male actor-stars transform physical appearances by changing hair colour or length, growing or removing facial hair, building muscle, and gaining or losing weight. As the male actor-star ages, physical changes naturally occur, yet still at some level he always remains recognizable. Over the duration of his film career Clooney's face has gradually lined and his hair colour progressively greyed, yet he's remained recognizably Clooney. When adopting facial hair for *Confessions of a Dangerous Mind, Burn After Reading* (2008), *The Men Who Stare at Goats* (2009) or *The Monuments Men*, he is constantly visible. On this note, *Syriana* (2005) is an interesting example to consider, for the portrayal of Bob Barnes, a veteran CIA operative working in the Middle East, could be described as an 'anti-Clooney' Clooney performance. To play Barnes, Clooney physically denied his familiar appearance, partly hiding his face by sporting a full set of beard and moustache while adding 30 pounds to his waistline to bulk up and transform his body shape (Figure 2.1). Reshaping the body fits the larger scheme of the narrative, for Barnes/Clooney's pudgy out-of-shape figure attains meaning as a somatic metaphor for the film's message that field agents like Barnes hold no control or power in a political landscape so thoroughly shaped by petrodollars (see Chapter 4). Clooney's physical transformation for *Syriana* therefore demarcated differences attuned to the needs of the film. Even so, behind the facial hair and flab, Clooney was recognizably Clooney. Beyond appearances, playing a man who pushes back against the powerful institutional forces that would compromise his moral integrity, Clooney as Barnes is consistent with a familiar character type previously played by the actor-star in *Three Kings* and returned to in *Michael Clayton*.

Physical appearance grounds the star brand. As actor-stars mark their presence on-screen through bodily and vocal actions, however, it is necessary to consider matters of acting. Between different film roles, habitual repetition of a distinctive repertoire of facial expressions, gestures, poses, or ways of moving come to form a gestural 'signature' for the actor-star. Where the face achieves resemblance through what the actor-star looks like, these kinetic

Figure 2.1 The anti-Clooney Clooney. Heavyweight acting as Barnes in *Syriana* ('Syriana' directed by Stephen Gaghan © Warner Bros. Entertainment Inc. 2005. All rights reserved).

indicators create branded continuity through what the actor-star *does*. In Clooney's case, he has unified gesture, movement and speech to produce two broad acting modes respectively serving the needs of drama and comedy. Clooney's 'dramatic' mode is characterized by physical and vocal containment, keeping gestures close to the body and rarely moving or speaking with speed or flexibility. This is the mode most visible in the *Ocean's* trilogy, *Solaris* (2002), *Syriana, Good Night, and Good Luck, The Good German, Michael Clayton, Up in the Air, The American* (2010), *The Ides of March* and *The Descendants* (2011). Creating a relatively inert and vocally measured figure, this is a manner of acting designed to communicate cool and contained authority. Conversely, Clooney's 'comic' mode conveys humour through using the body and voice to act amusingly by striking attitudes disproportionate to the circumstances in play. This is most obvious in his tendency for 'mugging', using exaggerated or enlarged facial expressions and contortions for the purposes of comedic effect. This is the mode deployed in *O Brother, Where Art Thou?* (see pp. 59–68), *Intolerable Cruelty* (2003), *Leatherheads* and *Burn After Reading*. These modes belong within larger generic frameworks. So, when measured against everyday behaviour, the comic mode exceeds the norms of quotidian manners, but in the context of film comedy, such actions appear fully appropriate, preserving 'generic verisimilitude' (Neale 2000: 32). Clooney's comic mode plausibly conforms to the general conventions of comedy performance where the big or extravagant are permitted and expected. While in many of Clooney's films one or the other of these modes predominates, they are not mutually exclusive or generically pure, for, with cases like *Out of Sight, Three Kings, The Men Who Stare at Goats* or *Money Monster* (2016), Clooney's acting moves between both modes in a single act.

These modes are not unique to Clooney, for, shaped by broader generic frameworks, they represent ways of acting commonly shared with other actors. The modes are therefore important but not absolute definers of Clooney's branded distinctiveness. Instead, the actor-star's performative signature is to be discerned at a more precise level in actions particular to the one performer. Early in his career Clooney became known for his habitual repetition of a particular gestural 'tic' or mannerism: his tendency for dipping and jiggling his head at selected moments in his performances.[1] This action appears very briefly in moments when Clooney shakes and/or nods his head back and forth and side to side in a series of small rapid movements, occasionally concluding by dropping his head to one side. Although only a fleeting action, in the early years of Clooney's career, this tic became an all-purpose gesture, variously deployed to add emphasis to the spoken word, or to convey a character's irritation, exasperation, anger, or appreciation of comic irony. Over the four and a half years he was Doug Ross in *ER*, Clooney found plenty of occasions where the pathos or humour of a moment was best answered by jiggling his head. He then carried this gesture over to his film work. When Clooney was vying to be considered for the role of Archie Gates in *Three Kings*, reportedly director David O. Russell was only willing to accept the actor on condition Clooney contain the mannerisms he'd acquired during his TV work. 'I want you to be very still in this role', Russell told Clooney (quoted in Waxman 2005: 229). Russell spent time in pre-production attempting to coach Clooney's acting, but as the actor famously fell out with the director while working on the film, it may be doubtful how far Clooney heeded that advice. Once Clooney's movie career matured, the mannerism became less pronounced but never entirely disappeared. Instead it remains a signature feature of Clooney's acting, which is not confined to any genre but equally traverses his dramatic and comedic modes. During the finale of *Michael Clayton*, the gesture is used – albeit it only momentarily and in a rather subdued manner – to emphasize the anger of Clooney's honourable 'fixer' (the employee of a corporate law firm hired to make transgressions by the company's clients go away) as he ensnares a corporation's chief counsel Karen Crowder (Tilda Swinton), who is responsible for ordering the killing of his friend. It is also to be witnessed in *The Monuments Men*, communicating relaxed good humour as Clooney's character Frank Stokes saunters through a military training camp while Lieutenant Donald Jeffries (Hugh Bonneville) introduces him to the eclectic team of individuals he'll lead in recovering art treasures stolen by the Nazis. For *Money Monster*, the mannerism becomes part of a collection of gestures representing the swaggering arrogance of Lee Gates, host of a TV finance infotainment show, as he imparts investment tips to his audience. It may only be a small action but Clooney's head-jiggling encapsulates the tensions and paradoxes of star acting: on the one hand, the gesture is a sign of difference, motivated by specific narrative circumstances, yet on the other it also operates as a sign of continuity, a signature mannerism visible across other Clooney films.

Physical appearances and a gestural signature provide visible signs of the actor-star. With Clooney the voice equally, and maybe even more uniquely, operates to brand his acting. Few stars working in modern American cinema may be so immediately recognizable from their voice alone. One magazine profile described him as having 'one asset that's rare among modern actors: a distinctive, attractive roguish voice he knows how to exploit to sly effect' (Carson 2007: 116). Combining a deep, throaty timbre, occasionally verging on a growl, with a steady and deliberate pace, Clooney's voice communicates authoritative weight, control and ease regardless of what he is saying. It is a voice that has been described as making 'monotone speaking sensual', 'blend[ing] smooth and rough' (WatchMojo.com 2015) and maintaining a level register that has earned Clooney the label 'the master of the monotone' (ArgueLab. com 2015). This is, maybe, a misleading description: Clooney's voice does not have a monotonous lack of intonation, colour or variation; rather, mixing a low tone and steady pace creates a basic range – an oral foundation – that Clooney's voice consistently stays within. This depth and measured tempo ensures that whatever Clooney is saying, he communicates calm confidence and unfazed composure. This relaxed manner of speaking does not mean Clooney speaks in an informal, casual manner: there is no mumbling, slurring or hesitancy in his speech. Rather tone and pace combine with clarity of diction to relay a fluent and articulate commitment to the spoken word. To add emphasis to his speech, Clooney sometimes pauses mid-sentence or otherwise over-enunciates certain words. In Clooney's dramatic mode, the calm steadiness of his speech usually melds with physical containment to unite voice and body in conveying confident surety and grounded solidity. For the comic mode, however, facial and gestural excesses are accompanied by various vocal flourishes that depart from the foundational monotone. Against the usual well-regulated authoritative calm, raising the pitch and pace of the voice in this mode is used precisely to signal a breakdown of control, for example to perform moments of hysterical irritability or incredulous frustration.

It is the distinctiveness of the voice that gives Clooney a performing presence even when he is not visible on-screen. Clooney is unseen in the animated feature *South Park: Bigger, Longer & Uncut* (1999) but when the character of Kenny is admitted to hospital for burns treatment, Clooney's cameo voicing Dr Gouache is enough to set off a chain of intertextual associations extending back to *ER*. Likewise, for the animated feature *Fantastic Mr. Fox* (2009), Clooney is visually absent yet always present through his voicing of the eponymous character. In *Gravity* (2013), Clooney's character Matt Kowalski disappears from sight once he floats off into deep space, yet for a period he retains an unmistakable 'on-screen' presence as the actor's voice continues to instruct Sandra Bullock's character Ryan Stone in how to survive the catastrophic accident they've just experienced. At the very opening of *Money Monster*, the screen is still only showing production company credits when Clooney first enters through his voice narrating the workings of electronic trading in financial markets.

Voice is a key vehicle for branding Clooney's presence, yet it must be noted that for several territories in the world film market the voice of Clooney is not Clooney's own voice. In the 2016 documentary *Being George Clooney*, interviewees talk about their experiences of dubbing Clooney's voice for the release of his films in non-English-speaking markets. With dubbing, a significant component to star-acting becomes devolved to multiple others. In Germany alone, Detlef Bierstedt and Martin Umbach have both dubbed for Clooney on different occasions. Potentially this multiplication of vocal sources dissolves the branding weight of the star voice. Two factors ensure this is not the case, however. First, as performers repeatedly dub the voices for specific Hollywood actors, over time they become the 'designated' voice artists for particular territories. As these performers are regarded by audiences in national markets as the authentic sound of a star, in their own way dubbing artists become markers of branded continuity. Secondly, creative interpretation plays a significant part in the work of dubbing. Designated voice artists are not required to exactly imitate the sound of a star's voice but instead have the licence to produce a perceived fit between the voices they create and their understandings of the stars they dub. In Brazil, for example, Marco Antônio Costa explains that when dubbing Brad Pitt he adopts a soft tone but for Clooney has cultivated what he describes as an 'incorporated' and 'metallic' voice. Across large parts of the world film market, therefore, the Clooney voice is not the voice of the actor-star himself, but rather is the product of multiple others who each distinctively mix tone, pace and pitch to create their own branded interpretations of the authentic Clooney sound. Distinctive in their own ways, the voices created by designated dubbing artists multiply rather than dissolve the branding of the star voice, producing various subsidiary or associated articulations of the star brand. Across the international film market, Clooney's own voice is therefore just one branded iteration of the Clooney voice. As manifestly visible signs, physical appearance and gesture are the most evident pointers of the actor-star's branded presence. In Clooney's case, however, his voice makes him present even when the body is visually absent. At the same time, the interpretive work of dubbing decouples physicality and speech, so that the body may be present when the actor's voice is not.

As signs of Clooneyness, physical appearance, signature gestural tics, and distinctive vocal qualities all work in combination to brand and package the actor-star's performances. These are the markers of sameness that traverse the differences of individual characters. Having identified these branded indicators of Clooney, the remainder of this chapter uses the examples of *O Brother, Where Art Thou?* and *Ocean's Eleven* to examine how his acting negotiates the balance between narrative particularity and star similarity.

Acting funny in *O Brother, Where Art Thou?*

Two weeks after exiting *ER*, Clooney signed to work on *O Brother, Where Art Thou?*, written by brothers Ethan and Joel Coen, respectively the producer and director of the film. Jointly financed by Disney's Touchstone Pictures division and Universal, *O Brother* was made by the London-based production company Working Title, a subsidiary of Universal Studios (Fleming 1999a). Set in 1937 during the Great Depression, this period comedy tells the story of three convicts who escape a prison chain gang to embark on a journey across rural Mississippi. Clooney's character, Ulysses Everett McGill, lures fellow inmates Delmar O'Donnell and Pete Hogwallop, played by Tim Blake Nelson and John Turturro, to join him in the breakout with the promise of retrieving the spoils of the armoured car hold-up he says landed him in jail. This is only a deception, however, for there is no buried hoard, and McGill spun the armoured car story as bait to persuade the others to escape – after all, he is chained to them. Instead the true goal is to get out so he can stop his ex-wife

Penny, played by Holly Hunter, marrying another man. During their journey the escapees meet up with blues guitarist Tommy Johnson (Chris Thomas King) and, posing as bluegrass group the Soggy Bottom Boys, the quartet make a recording of the old-time country standard 'Man of Constant Sorrow' that, unbeknown to them, becomes a local hit.

Close analysis of bodily and vocal actions illustrates the manners that have characterized Clooney's comic mode of performance. After they escape, McGill/Clooney, O'Donnell/Blake Nelson and Hogwallop/Turturro make their way across country and their journey is documented through a montage of shots. In the trio's first full scene, as part of their getaway they try to board a moving freight train while chained together. McGill/Clooney climbs into a boxcar but finds it already occupied by four stony-faced hobos. He is in the process of enquiring whether they can free him and his companions from their chains when Hogwallop/Turturro, who is still outside and running alongside the train, trips and falls to the ground beside the tracks dragging the others with him by the chain. With this scene, Clooney's acting is integrated into four systems of meaning: narrative, genre, auteurim and stardom. First, Clooney's body and voice perform the practical work of advancing McGill's story and the overall narrative. Through physical action and speech, Clooney's acting serves the needs of the narrative by enacting character agency. He runs alongside the boxcar, scrambles aboard, speaks to the hobos, and then falls on his stomach as he is dragged outside. Secondly, Clooney's acting is attuned to the conventions of genre. *O Brother* provides an example of Clooney using physical and vocal exaggeration to perform in his comic mode. As he runs alongside the train, McGill/Clooney's facial expressions portray both gritted-teeth determination and wide-eyed desperation (Figure 2.2). With this look, Clooney conveys a clash between the drama of escape and the comic absurdity of the moment. While the group are resolutely intent on getting away, at the same time it is an act of high foolishness for

Figures 2.2–2.5 Acting the genre. Clooney's comic mode of performance in *O Brother, Where Art Thou?* ('O Brother, Where Art Thou?' directed by Joel Coen © Touchstone Pictures and Universal Studios 2000. All rights reserved).

three guys chained together to try and scramble aboard a boxcar. Once McGill/Clooney has successfully boarded the car he cheerfully asks the occupants, 'Say, any of you boys smithies? Or, if not smithies per se, were you otherwise trained in the metallurgical arts before straitened circumstances forced you into a life of aimless wanderin'?' In part, the comedy here is a product of the script: McGill/Clooney's lines employ overly convoluted phrasing to ask a very straightforward question but also use ornate terms to communicate exaggerated respect and sympathy for the misfortunes of the hobos. Equally, the humour of the scene is an effect of acting. To ingratiate himself with the occupants of the car, McGill/Clooney's body and voice produce an overstated sense of bonhomie. He greets the hobos with a wide-eyed, open-mouthed look expressing a combination of surprise, friendship and the struggle to compose himself and catch his breath after the run (Figure 2.3). To present a welcoming manner, McGill/Clooney positions himself face on to his 'audience' of hobos, using open arm and hand gestures, and speaking with a buoyantly up-and-down cadence to his voice. McGill is improvising and thinking on the spot, and the sense that this is an opportunistic show of friendliness is underlined by how the framing and positioning present McGill/Clooney as if speaking on a stage (Figure 2.4). This performance is swiftly undermined, however, for before McGill/Clooney can get an answer to his question the scene turns to slapstick when Hogwallop/Turturro's fall yanks McGill/Clooney from his feet, and as he is dragged from the train on his stomach, his sense of alarm is conveyed by a startled look (Figure 2.5). Clooney's facial expressions, vocal lightness and brutal pratfall fit the specific needs of the scene while preserving generic convention.

For the scene, Clooney's body and voice create a push–pull effect between narrative and comedy, enacting the narrative necessity of McGill's determined intent to escape while also producing the comedic effect of showing the 'hero's' responses to having his ambitions thwarted in a most farcical manner. In this respect, the scene illustrates the general absurdist tone characterizing Clooney's acting. This is most evident in Clooney's mugging: his repeated use of exaggerated facial expressions for comedic effect. At various moments, while in the midst of ridiculous circumstances, Clooney pulls these showy expressions to communicate overstated irritability, anger or panic. Elsewhere in the film, they appear when communicating wounded annoyance to Hogwallop/Turturro and O'Donnell/Nelson after being pulled from the train (Figure 2.6); anxious urgency when hearing the distant barks of the sniffer dogs used by the search team hunting the escaped trio (Figure 2.7); alarm after the posse catch up with them (Figure 2.8); and hysterical terror as the trio escape a burning barn (Figure 2.9). A particularly condensed show of these manners comes when McGill/Clooney expresses disbelieving indignation to a store owner, who is not only unable to quickly obtain a replacement transmission belt for the car stolen by the trio, but even more frustratingly doesn't supply McGill's favourite Dapper Dan hair pomade (Figure 2.10). These facial gymnastics are just part of a larger scheme physicalizing Clooney's comic mode of performance. At later points, he uses his body to perform clownish gestures, including striking a caricatured pugilist pose to engage Penny's new 'suitor' Waldrip in a fist fight (Figure 2.11), or dancing like a fool while donning the flimsy disguise of a false beard as he and his companions perform 'Man of Constant Sorrow' in the film's finale (Figure 2.12).

Although certainly larger than life, these expressions and gestures are entirely appropriate and plausible for comedic acting. Beyond genre, however, Clooney's heightened comedic manners also create a fit with a third framework of meaning: auteurism. Given the collective inputs that go into film-making, no movie can ever be regarded as the product of any single creative vision. Combining the roles of writers, producers, directors and editors, however, the Coens exercised control over key elements of the film-making process for *O Brother* and the film holds strong tonal similarities with their other films. Although

Figures 2.11–2.12 Clooney's comedic body. Exaggerated physicality in *O Brother, Where Art Thou?* ('O Brother, Where Art Thou?' directed by Joel Coen © Touchstone Pictures and Universal Studios 2000. All rights reserved).

the duo have made crime thrillers (*Blood Simple* (1984), *Miller's Crossing* (1990), *No Country for Old Men* (2007)) and a Western (*True Grit* (2010)), arguably the Coens are best known for their comedies. Prior to *O Brother*, with *Raising Arizona* (1987), *Barton Fink* (1991), *The Hudsucker Proxy* (1994) and *The Big Lebowski* (1998) the Coens acquired a reputation for comedies with a decidedly idiosyncratic tone born of broadly drawn characters, frequently verging on the caricature, who move through absurdist narratives shaped by bizarre and implausibly coincidental events. Over time these characteristics earned the Coens the title of 'kings of quirky' (Shoup 2016). 'Every Coen film describes a world so thoroughly conceived,' argues critic Jonathan Romney (2000), 'that each one is its own fictional micro-climate'. This is evident in the case of *O Brother*, for rather than attempting any recognizably realist depiction of Depression-era America, the film offers a world of its own creation populated almost entirely by oddballs. To present this bizarre population, the film's cast produce an acting spectrum ranging across varying degrees of eccentricity. At the most extreme end are the caricatured bodily and vocal manners used by Turturro and Nelson to depict Hogwallop and O'Donnell. At the opposite end are Johnson/King and Penny/Hunter, who both act in ways that are pretty much dramatically 'straight'. Clooney occupies the middle ground between these poles: his comic mode of performance is 'big' enough to seamlessly fit this eccentric world, yet when compared to Hogwallop/Turturro and O'Donnell/Nelson, he appears relatively restrained. In the train scene and throughout the film, Clooney's enactment of McGill creates a figure belonging to the quirky worlds and idiosyncratic character types commonly found in the comedies of the Coen brothers. With *O Brother*, Clooney's actor-star brand is inflected by the writer-producer-director brand of the brothers, with McGill presenting yet another Coenesque eccentric character creation. Clooney's enactment of McGill is not only shaped by conformance to generic verisimilitude but also by a kind of 'auteurist verisimilitude', formed of how the actor-star's body and voice are fully integrated into the idiosyncratic, quirky worlds of Coen comedies. It is a rendition that belongs to a seam of comedic performance in Clooney's career firmly linked to the Coens, for after *O Brother* he teamed up with the brothers for the comedies *Intolerable Cruelty*, *Burn After Reading* and *Hail, Caesar!*

Clooney acts in a mode markedly different from the performances he gives in *The Perfect Storm* and *Ocean's Eleven*, the two films that respectively precede and follow *O Brother*. McGill is a singular character creation belonging to the exact circumstances of a distinct narrative world. Still, as the performance in *O Brother* draws on familiar signs of Clooneyness, it intersects with a fourth framework of meaning by creating the distinctive similarities that enact the star brand. At all points in the film Clooney looks and sounds like Clooney. Compulsively greasing and combining his hair narrativizes McGill's obsessive styling but also draws attention to hair as a distinctive marker of Clooneyness. Certainly, Clooney's mugging in *O Brother* fits the film's generic and auteurist frameworks, but equally creates a point of continuity with his performances in other films. Likewise, the habit of head-jiggling occasionally appears: it is there when McGill/Clooney first greets the hobos in the boxcar but then later when expressing frustration over the store owner's inability to supply his preferred hair pomade, responding to Hogwallop/Turturro's accusation that he has stolen a watch, or insisting to three of his young daughters that contrary to what their mother has told them, he wasn't killed in a train accident. Set in the Deep South, the film's cast vocally play up the region's twang and drawl for comic effect but Clooney makes no such concessions; instead his voice retains its familiar sound. For comic inflection or to convey emotion, on occasions Clooney raises his vocal pitch and quickens his rate of speaking, yet never departs for any extended period from his usual foundational deep tone.

With multiple references to Homer's epic poem *The Odyssey* and using a title lifted from the 1941 Preston Sturges film comedy *Sullivan's Travels*, *O Brother* exemplifies the Coens' postmodern tendency for intertextual allusion.[2] As the film's various cultural references don't actually inflect the narrative, their significance lies in making appeals to cinephilic knowingness. Clooney fits into this allusive play. Going on the run, it is plausible that McGill should be unshaven, yet the longer, darker stubble on Clooney's top lip gives the appearance of a moustache. When combined with his heavily slicked hair, Clooney's appearance loosely pastiches Clark Gable (Figure 2.13). No reference is ever explicitly made to this resemblance but it was widely noted by reviewers. For example, in the trade press *Variety*'s Todd McCarthy (2000: 32) believed Clooney

Figure 2.13 Retro-stardom. Clooney pastiches Gable in *O Brother, Where Art Thou?* ('O Brother, Where Art Thou?' directed by Joel Coen © Touchstone Pictures and Universal Studios 2000. All rights reserved).

was again 'recalling Clark Gable in his looks and line delivery'. Sheila Johnston (2000) of *Screen International* wrote, 'Clooney delivers a delightfully self-mocking comic performance as a smooth, mustachioed type with an addiction to hair pomade and flowery rhetoric and more than a passing resemblance to Clark Gable.' Writing in the alternative press for *New Times Los Angeles*, Robert Wilonsky (2000: 33) described Clooney's appearance in the film as 'a modern-day Clark Gable hiding behind a grinning facade and beneath hair so slicked back with pomade it weighs him down'. With *O Brother*, Wilonsky believed Clooney had 'become a movie star, and the Coens have given him his very own *It Happened One Night*'. By evoking old Hollywood, the enactment of McGill contributes to the nostalgic meanings of the Clooney brand. Using a star of conglomerate Hollywood to 'cite' a star of classic Hollywood, *O Brother* helped build the aura of nostalgia that became progressively attached to the Clooney brand (see the Introduction). *O Brother* shows how the branding of Clooney's acting comes not only from how he creates links to his own performances but also from how he enacts a reference point to male stars of another era.

Balancing difference with similarity, Clooney in *O Brother* is positioned within the contradictory dynamics that brand the acting of the actor-star. Shaped by narrative particularity, generic conformity and auteurist peculiarity, Clooney's acting in *O Brother* responds to the specific needs of the individual film. Equally, it shares enough commonalities to create a performance that is conspicuously Clooneyish. His body and voice represent the specific circumstances of McGill's story while forever presenting the figure on-screen as Clooney.

Ocean's Eleven and the performance of cool

O Brother, Where Art Thou? opened in North America shortly before Christmas 2000. Barring Clooney's one-minute cameo scene at the very end of *Spy Kids*, released in March 2001, after *O Brother* nearly a whole year passed before his next leading performance appeared in cinemas. *Ocean's Eleven* rolled out internationally from early December 2001. *Ocean's* continued Clooney's working relationship with Warner Bros., established during his years on *ER*, and reunited him with Steven Soderbergh, his director on *Out of Sight* (see Chapter 1). Financed and distributed by Warner, *Ocean's Eleven* was co-produced by Jerry Weintraub Productions and Section Eight, the company formed by Clooney and Soderbergh the year before (see Chapter 3). *Ocean's Eleven* is a very loose remake of *Ocean's 11*, the 1960 crime comedy that featured the 'rat pack' of Frank Sinatra, Dean Martin, Sammy Davis Jr, Peter Lawford and Joey Bishop. In the film's opening scene, serial confidence trickster and fraudster Danny Ocean, played by Clooney, convinces a prison parole board to release him. Once out Ocean immediately recruits a crew of criminal accomplices to steal the contents of a banking vault holding gambling proceeds from three Las Vegas casinos owned by Terry Benedict (Andy Garcia), the man whom Ocean's wife Tess (Julia Roberts) is now romantically involved with. Together the team perform an elaborate heist that not only sees them successfully get away with Benedict's money but also enables Ocean to win back

Tess. Repeating a pattern already seen in Clooney's career, rather than a straight-out lead he is at the forefront of a core ensemble (see Chapter 1). This time, however, Clooney shared the screen with other major bankable names from Hollywood film. On-screen credits and posters both confirmed and refuted star hierarchies: five names – Clooney, Matt Damon, Garcia, Brad Pitt and Roberts – were separated from the remainder of the cast, and to avoid any clash of star egos, the surnames were ordered alphabetically (Figure 2.14).[3] Amid this ensemble, Clooney emerges as the star among the stars: not only does his name appear first in the alphabetical ordering of credits and on promotional materials, but as the movie title might suggest, Clooney's character is the central organizing driver of the narrative and consequently gets more screen time than anyone else.

Ocean's Eleven is significant to the enactment of the Clooney brand for a series of reasons. For *O Brother*, Clooney used his comic acting mode, but *Ocean's Eleven* illustrates use of the 'dramatic' mode. *Ocean's Eleven* contains plenty of humour but is without the high comedy of *O Brother*. Consequently, there is no evidence among the *Ocean's* cast of the caricaturing and slapstick seen in the Coen brothers' film. Appearing sequentially in Clooney's run of lead roles, the two films provide a point of contrast from which to compare how the voice and body are used to enact differences according to specific narrative circumstances and generic conventions. Compared to the mugging and twitchy manners used in *O Brother*, Clooney's performance of Ocean is notable for its stasis and calm. In voice and in body, Clooney performs a figure of contained control who fits with the movie's narrative world and generic credentials. Ocean's crew is made up of a cast of larger-than-life characters, and although the heist premise might suggest the film is a thriller, the complexity and extravagance of the measures taken to steal the money are implausibly absurd. With this light-hearted tone, *Ocean's Eleven* is best described as a heist caper. Clooney's acting fits this tone, for despite the unlikeliness of the narrative, his uses of the body

Figure 2.14 Star among stars. Clooney heads a stellar ensemble in a poster for *Ocean's Eleven* ('Ocean's Eleven' directed by Steven Soderbergh © Warner Bros. Entertainment Inc. 2001. All rights reserved).

and voice portray Ocean as someone who knows all and is always confident of success. The narrative context is far-fetched to the point of ridiculousness, yet Clooney acts dramatically straight as Ocean, a man carving out a steady path through whatever circumstances come his way. Ocean/Clooney is constantly calm and composed. Appearing nonchalant and relaxed while completely focused and determined, Clooney gives the characterization an overall quality of control. Clooney's acting in *Ocean's Eleven* could be summarized as a highly judged performance of cool.

But how does Clooney enact cool? *Ocean's Eleven* opens with a static medium shot of a wooden chair set centre frame inside a bare prison interior. Ocean/Clooney leisurely walks into shot, sits, faces frontwards, and is questioned by the parole board, whose members are positioned out of frame (Figure 2.15). These opening few seconds immediately establish Ocean's containment. Apart from greeting the board and giving his name, Clooney is at first silent, and other than a few eye movements, is entirely still. Asked to explain why he was implicated, though never charged, in a history of other confidence schemes and frauds preceding the incident for which he was imprisoned, Ocean/Clooney slightly adjusts himself in the chair, looks down at his hands, utters a faint 'tut', then brings his head up to face the board and pause before responding with, 'As you say ma'am, I was never charged'. This is his most mobile moment in the entire scene. Although the shift of position and tut implies irritation with the question, by returning to his former upright state and then speaking with an even, measured tone, Ocean/Clooney is shown gathering himself before presenting a polite, respectful and obedient front to the board. Quizzed over the reason for the (at this stage unspecified) crime that led to his conviction, he slightly pulls back in his chair, raises his shoulders, making a deep intake of breath, quickly looking off frame left, and then returns his look to the board and explains, 'my wife left me, I was upset, I got into a self-destructive pattern'. While the breath shows Ocean/Clooney disciplining

Figures 2.15–2.16 Enacting cool. Ocean/Clooney performs for the parole board in *Ocean's Eleven* ('Ocean's Eleven' directed by Steven Soderbergh © Warner Bros. Entertainment Inc. 2001. All rights reserved).

himself against succumbing to the emotional circumstances he is about to describe, the familiar level tone of the Clooney voice communicates calm restraint. Asked whether he'd likely fall back into a similar pattern if released, referring again to his wife, Ocean/Clooney responds, 'she already left me the once, I don't think she'd do it again just for kicks'. Though the script hints at resistive discomfort with both the interview and the wife's departure, Ocean/Clooney's maintenance of bodily and vocal composure keep any emotions under control. Shooting the conversation in a single static one-minute continuous long take underlines how Ocean/Clooney maintains level-headed composure. Towards the very end of the scene, Ocean/Clooney is asked, 'Mr Ocean, what do you think you would do if released?' and there is a cut to a close-up of Clooney's face. He does not vocalize a response but the reframing makes it possible to see the small visual detail of his mischievously cunning sideways glance, hinting at his full intention to return to crime and the wish to win back his wife (Figure 2.16).

In popular narrative film the entrance of the actor-star always has two effects: establishing character and introducing the star asset. In this opening scene, Clooney's body and voice enact Ocean's narrative: his expository backstory explaining why he's in prison, unhappiness with his wife's departure, and setting up Ocean's overall goal. According to the circumstances of the scene, Ocean wrestles with two sets of tensions: his resistance to institutional processes and the emotional pain of his wife's departure. Still, Clooney's show of bodily and vocal restraint see him keep his cool. At the same time, Clooney is presented as a figure of spectacle. Together the static shot, symmetric centralized framing, long take, cut to the close-up, frontwards placement of the performer's body, solitary occupancy of the frame, and measured vocal tone, all put Clooney on show as the film's central presence. The opening scene therefore represents Clooney as Ocean but also presents Clooney as Clooney.

Linking Clooney bodily and vocally to the character of Danny Ocean, acting is foundational to the performance of cool in *Ocean's Eleven*. But acting is only one element contributing to an overall enactment of cool creating Ocean and his world. At least two other elements add to this effect: costume and music. Costuming operates as a key system for defining Ocean/Clooney and his band of accomplices. For Jeffrey Kurland, costume designer on the film,

the inspiration came for the movie from the original rat pack ... Looking back into the '60s to what they look like was a very important, you know, piece of research because we wanted to emulate them without copying them, without, you know, repeating that, so my task was to take that look, that feeling, that was the rat pack of the '60s and move it up so that's what I set out to do and that's what Steven [Soderbergh] wanted to show. He wanted it heightened. You know. He wanted them, as he said, to sparkle.

(Academy Originals 2015)

While the costuming might have taken inspiration from *Ocean's 11*, the male styling in *Ocean's Eleven* bears only passing resemblance to the original. For most of *Ocean's 11*, Sinatra (Danny Ocean), Martin (Sam Harmon) and other members of the team are smartly dressed in shirts and ties with suits or sports jackets and tailored trousers. In the 'remake', only Ocean/Clooney comes close to that look. Ocean/Clooney wears a succession of suits, jackets and trousers, but accompanied by an open-collar shirt or roll-neck sweater. Alluding to but not copying the male costuming of *Ocean's 11*, Ocean/Clooney's styling should be seen as part of what Mark Gallagher (2013: 157) calls the '"neo-retro" sensibility' of *Ocean's Eleven*. In *Ocean's 11* there is a fair degree of uniformity to the styling of the male group but in *Ocean's Eleven* each member of the ensemble is distinctively dressed and costuming acts as an index for character differences. Ocean/Clooney's dress covers a muted colour palette of black, charcoal or light grey, navy blue, browns and white, and the mix of besuited formality with open-collar casualness gives him an air of cool, relaxed authority. As Ocean's second in command Rusty Ryan, Pitt also wears suits, smart jackets and trousers, but compared to Ocean/Clooney his appearance is more showy: silver-grey or beige ties, white double-breasted suit, patterned or iridescent wide-collared shirts in various colours, and a shiny leather jacket. If Ocean/Clooney appears 'sharp', Ryan/Pitt is 'flash'. As the young pickpocket Linus Caldwell, Matt Damon's casual attire gives him the appearance of an overgrown boy to communicate his status as the inexperienced naïve rookie, while the plain geekish non-style of Eddie Jemison stereotypically conveys the technological brilliance of his character Livingston Dell. The process of differentiating through dress extends across the entire central male ensemble but the styling of their differences is systematized. While members of the crew are highly individualized, each has an essential role to play in collectively completing the heist. Costume is therefore a statement of individual idiosyncrasies but at the same time creates a collective identity for the group. They may look unalike but idiosyncratic difference is the very thing that unites them.[4] Clooney's styling was fitted into this system. Kurland aimed to mark Ocean as 'the leader of the pack and the way in which his character is dressed I wanted to show that this is the top of the pyramid where everything trickles down from so the style that is Danny Ocean is a very important style because it is the catalyst for what everybody else looks like'. The central male ensemble is therefore sartorially defined around Ocean/Clooney's style.

Music also contributes to the over-arching 'hip' tone, producing an atmosphere of cool that pervades the narrative world Ocean/Clooney inhabits. 'Found' music, in the form of pre-existing popular recordings from the 1950s, 1960s and 1980s, is juxtaposed with an original soundtrack by the Irish musician, DJ and producer David Holmes.[5] For *Ocean's Eleven*, Holmes constructed a sound that is unmistakably modern while belonging to a former era with influences from jazz, funk and the film or television soundtracks of Lalo Schifrin (particularly *Mission: Impossible* (1966–73), *Bullitt* (1968), *Dirty Harry* (1971) and *Enter the Dragon* (1973)). These musical reference points don't fix the film in time but rather evoke an unspecified pastness that further contributes to the production of a cool neo-retro feel. Holmes had already used a similar music design when working with Soderbergh and Clooney on *Out of Sight*, and after *Ocean's Eleven*, he repeated the formula when reuniting with the director and actor-star for the two sequels *Ocean's Twelve* (2004) and *Ocean's Thirteen* (2007). From *Out of Sight* to *Ocean's Thirteen*, for nearly a decade Holmes's music effectively became the 'sound of Clooney', the soundtrack to the brand. Using music in these ways not only gives *Out of Sight* and the *Ocean's* trilogy one foot in the past but also enhances the nostalgic connotations of the Clooney brand, creating a neo-retro world for the actor-star to move through.

Combinations of acting, costume and music enact Ocean/Clooney's overall performance of cool. After the opening scene with the parole board, for example, there follows a transformation sequence with Ocean/Clooney passing through a montage of moments, as he walks through the prison, is returned his personal possessions, exits the prison, and turns up in an Atlantic City casino where he takes a seat at a blackjack table. Like any transformation sequence, this montage plays out the production of identity. While interviewed by the board, Ocean/Clooney is dressed in a prison uniform with his thick hair swept back and sporting a circle beard. As he is processed for release, Ocean/Clooney appears in a dress suit, dress shirt, with a bow tie casually undone around his neck (Figure 2.17), before leaving through the prison gates clad in a smart, tailored overcoat. As these are the clothes he was presumably wearing when arrested, besuited formality represents Ocean's natural state. Arriving in Atlantic City, Ocean/Clooney rides up an escalator to enter the casino floor. He has changed again and this time is clean-shaven with his hair trimmed, and is wearing a range of coordinated browns including a causal but exceedingly smart sports jacket. Clooney stands erect yet the relaxed manner with which his right hand is loosely placed in the pocket of his trousers communicates casual, comfortable physicality. As Ocean/Clooney rises on the escalator, the camera is placed in a fixed position on the floor at the top of the stairs. With this framing, Ocean/Clooney appears to ride into frame, so that the shot, while static, seems to move downwards, gradually taking in his body and attire. In one sense this is a moment of simple narrative action: Ocean enters a casino. In another it is a staged moment of spectacle, performing a double act of becoming, for now cleaned up and dressed up Ocean/

Figures 2.17–2.18 Becoming Ocean and Clooney. The transformation sequence in *Ocean's Eleven* ('Ocean's Eleven' directed by Steven Soderbergh © Warner Bros. Entertainment Inc. 2001. All rights reserved).

Clooney not only reveals the look that will characterize him for the remainder of the film but also discloses a familiar vision of Clooney.

There is no speech during the sequence but instead Holmes's track 'Rodney Yates' forms a musical bridge across time and space.[6] With a characteristic mix of old and new, the track samples 'MSP' from jazz drummer Chico Hamilton's 1968 album *The Gamut*, layering this with a deep bass riff and electro keyboards. The track commences at the end of the parole board scene, just at the moment Ocean/Clooney is asked what he'd do if released and gives his sly look in close-up. With the track then following

Ocean/Clooney as he exits the prison and arrives in Atlantic City, it effectively becomes 'his' music. At the end of the scene with the board, Ocean/Clooney doesn't speak but the music, together with his sly look, articulates his response. As situated in this narrative context, the music becomes an index of Ocean's roguish disposition. The regularity of the drums and the bass riff create a rhythm that gives the track a driving momentum. This is underscored by Clooney's acting, where apart from the moment he stands at a table to inspect his personal belongings – nothing more than his wedding ring – he is always steadily moving forward. The track does not issue from any source within the on-screen narrative world but accompanies Ocean/Clooney on his journey across spaces. It belongs to him: he is the music and the music is him; where he goes, the music goes. As the track does not reappear in the film, it doesn't function as a repeated character theme, yet still it articulates the spirit of Ocean. From prison to casino, the rhythmic regularity of the music integrates with the even pace of Ocean/Clooney's walk to present a figure with a set purpose and clear sense of direction. As he leisurely strides through the casino, head held up, hands in his pockets, and seemingly inextricably accompanied by cool sounds, Ocean/Clooney presents a composed figure moving through space with absolute effortless confidence (Figure 2.18). In this short sequence, movement, deportment, costuming and music all combine to present Ocean/Clooney as smooth but resolute.

This production of cool by no means typifies the entirety of Clooney's output. It was there with *Out of Sight* and partially in evidence with *Three Kings* (1999) but then absent for *The Perfect Storm* and *O Brother*. Immediately following *Ocean's Eleven*, it was also missing from *Solaris* and Clooney's supporting roles in *Welcome to Collinwood* (2002) and *Confessions of a Dangerous Mind*. Beyond the *Ocean's* sequels, however, there are similarities with Clooney's performances in *The Good German, Michael Clayton, Up in the Air,*

The American, The Ides of March and *The Monuments Men*. A final
reason for why *Ocean's Eleven* and the other films in the trilogy are
significant is, then, how they collectively created a version of Clooney
that became the defining statement of the star brand. This was both a
symbolic and an economic effect. Repeating a single character across
the trilogy of *Ocean's* films with an accompanying performance
mode created a collection of meanings that, although limited to only
a few films, became the key articulation of the Clooney brand. The
significance of that enactment was then reinforced by the commercial
performance of the *Ocean's* series. Beginning its international rollout
in North America on 7 December 2001, *Ocean's Eleven* was one of
two major tentpole releases from Warner Bros. for the Christmas
holiday season.[7] Grossing over $183 million at the North American
theatrical box office, the film picked up a further $267 million in
ticket sales internationally to end with a worldwide total of nearly
$451 million. *Ocean's Twelve* and *Ocean's Thirteen* capitalized on that
success, reuniting Clooney, Soderbergh, Holmes, Jerry Weintraub
Productions, Section Eight and Warner Bros. to form a star/director/
music/genre/production companies/financier–distributor package
that led to the sequels respectively grossing nearly $363 million and
$311 million worldwide. With a cumulative worldwide box office
of over $1 billion, the *Ocean's* trilogy is the standout commercial
statement of Clooney's career. Among films in which Clooney has
taken a lead role, *Ocean's Eleven* remains the highest grossing and
the sequels occupy second and fourth positions (see Chapter 3).[8]
Ocean's Eleven and the subsequent instalments in the trilogy are
therefore foundational to the meaning and commercial status of the
Clooney brand. Clooney's performance of cool may not characterize
the whole of his output, yet it holds greater weight in expressing
and disseminating the actor-star's brand. For many members of the
global film audience, it is likely that their most familiar, and maybe
even their only, acquaintance with Clooney is through seeing him
as Danny Ocean. Between *O Brother* and *Ocean's Eleven*, Clooney's

modes of acting are quite different, yet in their respective ways each is stylistically alike to performance manners used in other films. Both modes are therefore formative to the Clooney brand, yet the performance of cool enacted in *Ocean's Eleven* became the most commercially successful and popularly known, representing the predominant definition of the actor-star brand.

Conclusion

Dressed in a dark suit and crew-neck sweater with his short hair neatly side-parted, Clooney casually walks up to the door of an apartment where a party is taking place and rings the doorbell. The scene is accompanied by the cool Latin sound of 'Night Over Manaus', a 2001 release from Boozoo Bajou that sampled the 1963 recording 'O Morro Nao Tem Vez' from bossa nova pioneer and one-time Sinatra collaborator Antônio Carlos Jobim. When the hostess answers the door, she greets Clooney with 'Oh, George'. Slightly jiggling his head, Clooney responds 'ciao'. But as Clooney has arrived without any alcohol, the hostess must tell him, 'No Martini. No party', and closes the door on him. Soon he returns with multiple cases of the drink (clooneyfiles 2007).

It's another occasion and this time Clooney, dressed in black suit and shirt, again with his hair tidily parted, is about to seduce a woman in his apartment when the couple are interrupted by the sound of music and popping corks from a party upstairs. When he goes upstairs, the party hostess greets him with 'George', and he gains admittance by bringing a bottle of Martini. The party may be a very twenty-first-century event but the partygoers are moving to KC and the Sunshine Band's 1977 hit 'I'm Your Boogie Man'. Clooney circles the room, taking glasses from all the guests, and as he exits the door with a trolley full of bottles, he lightly admonishes the revellers with 'No Martini. No party' (heynothinyoucansay 2008).

Walking down a street dressed in charcoal grey suit and black turtleneck, Clooney enters an outlet for the upmarket coffee system Nespresso. He catches the eye of a woman sitting with her female friend. As Clooney prepares himself a coffee, he overhears the pair saying 'dark', 'very intense', 'balanced', 'unique', 'mysterious', 'an intense body', 'delicate and smooth', 'with a strong character', 'rich', 'very rich' and 'deep and sensual'. Smugly taking pleasure in the presumption they are speaking about him – although surprised to hear one of the women state 'I would say Latin American' – Clooney smiles to himself, rocks his head to the side, raises his eyebrows, and goes over to the women. Just as he's about to introduce himself, he hears 'and a delicious aftertaste', and realises the true nature of their conversation. 'You're talking about Nespresso, right?' Clooney asks, and when the women confirm it is the coffee that is moving them, he regretfully acknowledges, 'Yeah', dipping his head to quickly cover the embarrassment of his own conceit, answering with a knowing 'What else?' accompanied by a slight laugh and smile before leaving (Rockonjuju 2006).

These spot advertisements, aired on UK television, are just a few of the product commercials Clooney has appeared in. He did whole series of spot ads for Martini and Nespresso, along with television and/or print campaigns for Fiat and Honda cars, Police sunglasses, Lancelot whisky, Norwegian financial services group DnB, and Omega watches. When featured in advertising, Clooney has not represented a character but instead appears as 'himself', recognizing that in this context the self is of course a performance. With the Martini and Nespresso ads, all the familiarized physical signs of Clooneyness are there: the jawline, short and neat hair, head-jiggling and growling voice. Did he not look so obviously like Clooney, the party hostesses might not be able to immediately recognize him as 'George'. With these ads, it doesn't matter what the product is, Clooney constantly appears in suits accompanied by soundtracks borrowing from the past.[9] Self-conscious use in these commercials of Clooney's informalized but smart styling draw on his off- and on-screen identities. Off-screen, photographs of Clooney in the celebrity press have frequently shown him leaving restaurants or attending film festivals or other events wearing suits with casual shirts. On-screen, the commercials presented Clooney in the image of Danny Ocean. Off- and on-screen identities were therefore blurred, for even when appearing to act himself, Clooney was Ocean and Ocean was Clooney. Any distinction between actor and character was elided to form a package of cool smoothness.

Star or celebrity endorsements operate a promotional logic whereby a transfer of meanings is created between product and star, with star and product mutually signifying one another (McDonald 2013: 59–63). The Martini and Nespresso campaigns capitalized on the look, movement and vocal tone characterizing Clooney's Clooneyness. Combining Clooney's performance of cool charm with his slightly self-deprecating sense of humour, the campaigns imported the meanings of upmarket class and sophistication to promote a ready-mixed cocktail and instant coffee pods. Using the look and movement of the actor-star brand is prevalent in star product endorsements but in other cases the transfer of meanings takes an entirely aural form. One 2005 television commercial told viewers:

This is the famous Budweiser beer. We know of no other brand produced by any other brewer which costs so much to brew and age. Our exclusive beechwood aging produces a taste, a smoothness and a drinkability you'll find in no other beer at any price. This is Budweiser. This is beer.

(CERVECERIA SCHOPPEN 2013)

Here a transference of brand meanings was constructed as a 'famous' beer was lent meaningful gravitas through the masculine authority imparted by the deep, steady and distinctive tone of the Clooney voice.

As Clooney's fame is founded on his feature film and television work, his advertising work might appear of minor or peripheral importance. Yet looking at star endorsements provides a valuable route into understanding the connection between branded performance and commerce that is fundamental to film stardom. For his television advertising work, Clooney used his body and voice to enact an easily recognizable set of meanings and effects. The TV spot adverts didn't attempt to import the entirety of Clooney's feature film persona or personas. Rather, they selectively worked with one specific version of Clooney familiar from the *Ocean's* trilogy. Clooney enacted a highly recognizable and commercially successful version of Clooneyness to create performances explicitly designed to sell things. Directly linking acting to commerce, star endorsements therefore make obvious the economic logic of branded performance. That logic is active in feature films but product endorsements more overtly foreground the branded performance of the actor-star as the outcome of repeated bodily and vocal markers used as signs of value in capitalist systems of exchange. To emphasize the place of actor-stars in film economics, stars are sometimes described as commodities, but it is mistaken to read star performance in these terms. As all systems of commercial transaction in film culture are set up for customers to pay for the film, consumers cannot directly buy a star performance. Film stars are therefore not commodities but rather a means for selling a certain category of cultural commodity: the feature film. Still, this does mean the branded performances of actor-stars operate as signs of commercial value. With the following chapter, the discussion therefore moves on to situate Clooney as a figure produced in the industrial environment of conglomerate Hollywood, and to consider the value of that figure in the film market.

Notes

1 For a humorous compilation of clips illustrating this gesture see ACTING!!! (2014).

2 Numerous allusions are made to Homer's classic tale. For example, Ulysses, the first name of Clooney's character, is a nod to the Latin form of Homer's hero Odysseus, and Penny is the diminutive of Penelope, Odysseus' wife. On their travels, McGill/Clooney, Hogwallop/Turturro and O'Donnell/Nelson meet a 'blind prophet' in the form of a railroad worker, a trio of singing 'sirens' washing clothes in a river, and a 'cyclops' who manifests as Big Dan Teague (John Goodman), a one-eyed Bible seller. In *Sullivan's Travels*, a fictional Hollywood film director, well known for his output of light comedies, hopes to attain artistic legitimacy by making 'O Brother, Where Art Thou?', a serious and socially relevant film about the Great Depression (Adams 2015: 134–40).

3 For a movie star in-joke, the film's end titles include the credit 'introducing Julia Roberts as Tess'. Throughout the previous decade, Roberts had been the most bankable female name in Hollywood, and just the year before had appeared in the Soderbergh-directed *Erin Brockovich* (2000) for which she'd reportedly received $20 million, the highest sum paid to a female star at that time (McDonald 2013: 142).

4 Costume also coheres the central male ensemble in a further way, for 'performing' the heist requires several members of the group to dress up by wearing costumes and adopting disguises. At various points Ryan/Pitt assumes the necessary attire to masquerade as a police officer, doctor and SWAT team member. To get the job done Frank Catton (Bernie Mac) works undercover in the casino as a dealer, while Caldwell/Damon becomes a Nevada Gaming Commission inspector, Dell/Jemison dresses as a casino technician, and old con Saul Bloom (Carl Reiner) is fitted with a bespoke suit to assume the fake identity of mysterious arms dealer 'Lyman Zerga'. With the brothers, Virgil and Turk Malloy (Casey Affleck and Scott Caan), their entire role in the heist is to dissemble by playing gamblers, bodyguards, room service porters and casino guards.

5 The found tracks include Perry Como 'Papa Loves Mambo' (1954), Percy Faith and His Orchestra 'Theme for Young Lovers' (1963), Elvis Presley 'A Little Less Conversation' (1968), Norman Greenbaum 'Spirit in the Sky' (1969) and Berlin 'Take My Breath Away' (1986).

6 The track had previously appeared on Holmes's 1997 album *Let's Get Killed*.

7 The other was *Harry Potter and the Philosopher's Stone* (2001) (aka *Harry Potter and the Sorcerer's Stone*).

8 *The Perfect Storm* ($329 million worldwide) is the third highest grossing. Selling over $723 million in tickets worldwide, *Gravity* achieved a higher gross than any installment in the *Ocean's* trilogy, although in a film where only three actors feature on-screen, Clooney remained very much secondary and subordinate to Sandra Bullock.

9 An original composition for Nespresso's 2006 UK TV campaign, Benjamin Raffaelli and Frédéric Doll's 'The Boutique' is reminiscent of the retro soundscape from Holmes's soundtracks for the *Ocean's* trilogy.

3 FLEXIBLE STARDOM: INDEPENDENCE/ HOLLYWOOD

Clooney's stardom intersects with the broad range of production contexts characterizing the industrial landscape of contemporary American film and television. As discussed in Chapter 1, during the 1980s Clooney worked on feature films made and released outside of Hollywood by independent production and distribution companies, while at the same time taking bit parts and supporting roles in television series for the major television networks. Five years on *ER* (1994–2009) brought Clooney into Hollywood, building up a lengthy association with Warner Bros. at the same time as he took leading roles for films from other Hollywood majors. Subsequently, Clooney then pursued a film career conducted almost entirely inside Hollywood. Like all contemporary Hollywood stars, Clooney has enjoyed independent status. Despite a long-term relationship with Warner, Clooney's services are not tied exclusively to any one company; rather he freely moves between acting assignments for the majors. Inside Hollywood, Clooney has worked across the full range of production models operated by the majors, from high-cost event movie spectaculars designed to appeal to large, popular audiences, to more modestly budgeted 'specialized' films aimed at smaller, limited audiences. Clooney is very aware of the artistic autonomy he enjoys:

As long as I'm able to say to the studio, 'We're going to do *Ocean's Twelve*, but I want to be able to do *Syriana* and some other films you guys aren't going to want to do,' I feel as if that's okay.

(quoted in Foundas 2005: 32)

This autonomy also extends beyond acting. The extent and presence of the Clooney brand has expanded as he's joined the 'Hollywood hyphenates' by multiplying his creative roles to become an actor-director-producer-writer through his independent production companies Section Eight and Smokehouse. Clooney's film career has therefore seen him not only moving between the independent sector and Hollywood but also moving independently inside Hollywood.

Negotiating a path across different production contexts and creative roles, Clooney is representative of 'flexible stardom', the adaptive and strategic movement of elite freelance actors who work across media, hire their services out to various employers, appear in films made and circulated by different models of production and distribution, and whose commercial value is deployed across varying tiers of the film market (McDonald 2017). The previous chapter discussed how the performance of smooth, controlled, effortless cool on-screen defined the Clooney brand, and that performance carries over to his status as an industry 'player'. Liberally moving across the industrial space of modern Hollywood, Clooney's mobility has become part of his branded identity. Just as Danny Ocean in *Ocean's Eleven* (2001) seems able to do and achieve anything, Clooney freely and smoothly moves across the business of modern Hollywood, comfortably and confidently acting across a diverse range of film projects, at the same time as directing and producing films, and running his own company.

Situating this industry 'performance', this chapter sees Clooney as a product of and a product in the business and market for Hollywood film. Positioning Clooney's flexible stardom in the context of conglomerate Hollywood, the chapter sees how Clooney has traversed tensions between independence and Hollywood from four directions: the structural organization of the contemporary American film industry; the status of independent stars in conglomerate Hollywood; the dispersal of the Clooney brand across different segments of the film market; and the workings of the star-based independent production company.

Hollywood, independents and Indiewood

Broadly divided between concentrations of corporate power and dispersed autonomous operations, historically the American film industry 'has been driven ... by the dual impulses of consolidation and independence' (Schatz 2013: 127). In the 1930s and 1940s, the core of Hollywood was defined by five major vertically integrated production-distribution-exhibition corporations, together with three smaller companies that functioned as producer-distributors or just as a distributor. From the late 1940s and into the 1950s, US anti-trust law forced the vertical disintegration of the majors, yet the industry consolidated once again as successive waves of conglomeration changed their ownership. Now six firms, all subsidiaries of larger diversified parent companies, represent the core of conglomerate Hollywood: Paramount Pictures Corporation, Sony Pictures Entertainment Inc., 20th Century Fox Film Corporation, Universal City Studios LLC, Warner Bros. Entertainment Inc., and Walt Disney Studios Motion Pictures. Outside this core, the business is populated by a wide array of independent companies – producers, distributors, exhibitors and many categories of service provider. Certainly, the business has always had a fair share of independent producers, distributors and exhibitors, yet historically there has never been any pure or absolute divide between Hollywood and the independents: producers from outside Hollywood have made films financed and/or released by the majors, while independent exhibitors have relied on releases from multiple suppliers, including the Hollywood majors. Rather than discreet segregation, Hollywood and independents have always co-existed in conditions of interaction, integration and co-dependence.

Clooney's stardom is a product of this independence/Hollywood dialectic. Starting his film career in productions made and released by independents, even once Clooney had established himself in Hollywood, he continued to appear in films made by many independent companies who received finance and distribution services from the majors (see the Filmography). To take one example: producer Paula Weinstein's Baltimore Spring Creek Productions already held a production agreement with Warner Bros. when in October 1996 the company paid a six-figure sum for movie rights to Sebastian Junger's non-fiction novel *The Perfect Storm: A True Story of Men Against the Sea*, due for publication the following May (Cohen 2000; Fleming 1996; Junger 2000). Junger's book creatively tells the true-life story of how, in 1991, the fishing-boat *Andrea Gail* and its crew disappeared without trace during a catastrophic storm (Junger 2000). From early 1998, Wolfgang Petersen's Radiant Productions also began partnering with Baltimore and Warner Bros. in developing the project, and in November that year Petersen was confirmed as director (Fleming 1998b; Karon and Petrikin 1998). Weinstein steered the project through the early stages of development before handing over to Petersen who apparently envisioned the film as a combination of *On the Waterfront* (1954) and *Twister* (1996) (Cohen 2000). Warner Bros. were reportedly keen to cast Nicolas Cage or Mel Gibson as Billy Tyne, captain of the ill-fated vessel, but both passed on the project and in May 1999 Clooney signed for the part (*The Hollywood Reporter* 1999; Fleming 1999b; Kit 1999a). After just finishing his fifth and final series of *ER*, Clooney's casting was based on the positive buzz that preceded Warner Bros.' release of *Three Kings* (1999). Warner Bros. funded the independents Spring Creek and Radiant to make *The Perfect Storm* before releasing the film domestically and in key international territories through its own theatrical distribution division. *The Perfect Storm* is therefore representative of a common model operating in modern Hollywood, whereby one of the majors provides finances and distributes a film, while devolving the actual task of film-making to independents.

Intersections between the majors and independents are endemic to Hollywood history but during the 1990s any distinction between the two became particularly blurred with the emergence of 'Indiewood', that part of the business 'in which Hollywood and the independent sector merge or overlap' (King 2005: 1). In the same decade as Clooney was establishing his name in television and film, the Hollywood majors either acquired leading independent producer-distributors (e.g. New Line and Miramax) or otherwise established their own subsidiaries (e.g. Sony Pictures Classics (SPC), Fox Searchlight, and Warner Independent Pictures (WIP)). Indiewood therefore emerged from the structural diversification of modern Hollywood, for 'the rise of conglomerate Hollywood involved not only the acquisition of the majors studios but also the annexation of key functions of the indie movement by a new breed of media giants' (Schatz 2013: 127). While granted a fair degree of operational autonomy, prevailing conditions of ownership meant the Indiewood subsidiaries could never be described as 'independent' in any meaningful way. Part of Hollywood and yet not Hollywood, Indiewood therefore complicated the meaning of 'independence' (Tzioumakis 2013).

Indiewood subsidiaries have released films across the spectrum of popular and niche tastes but acquired a reputation for handling the types of product targeting the market for so-called 'specialized film'. A vague, slippery term that has become something of a catch-all label for various forms of production and taste outside the mainstream (recognizing 'mainstream' itself remains an ambiguous descriptor) one definition classifies specialized as foreign-language films, feature documentaries, and archive or classic films, but also films without clear generic credentials, an innovative or unconventional aesthetic or narrative style, or that otherwise include 'complex and challenging subject matter' (BFI n.d.). Like populist cinema the primary purpose of speciality film remains the need to entertain. Speciality entertainment is distinguished from the popular by its aim to deliver a certain quality of entertainment, with 'quality' meaning not only a set of stylistic and narrative features but also a measure of aesthetic and intellectual distinction. Speciality film is 'arty', 'thoughtful', 'important' or 'deeper' amusement. This is not to say speciality film is unremittingly earnest and sombre but, when humour is present, it appears as 'clever' comedy in the form of quirky, offbeat or eccentric takes on life. Situated between mainstream popularity and avant garde elitism, speciality film appeals to a middlebrow sensibility. Rightly or wrongly, if the popular market is still presumed to be predominantly composed of teenagers and young adults, specialised film is regarded as addressing an older adult demographic of professionals, probably college educated. As speciality films are regarded as presenting an alternative to Hollywood, it is paradoxical that Indiewood should be a source of such films. In their various ways, the films that emerge from these intersections between Hollywood and the speciality sector become examples of 'quality Hollywood' (King 2016), 'serious Hollywood' (Baumann 2007: 18) or the 'smart film' (Sconce 2002).

Indiewood subsidiaries have released several films featuring Clooney. Three years after its acquisition by Disney, Miramax produced and distributed *From Dusk Till Dawn* (1996) and later *Confessions of a Dangerous Mind* (2002), while Miramax's own genre distribution subsidiary, Dimension, handled *Spy Kids* (2001) and *Spy Kids 3-D: Game Over* (2003) for the children's market. Universal's Focus Features produced and distributed *Burn After Reading* (2008) and *The American* (2010), while WIP and Fox Searchlight made and released, respectively, *Good Night, and Good Luck* (2005) and *The Descendants* (2011). Although part of the majors, Indiewood divisions have released or made the types of film more readily associated with certain examples of independent production and distribution.

With the exception of the *Spy Kids* movies, which were overtly aimed at the popular children's market, the Clooney Indiewood films are representative of this sub-sector. Mixing gun crime thriller and vampire horror, *From Dusk Till Dawn* self-consciously creates an abrupt clash of genres (see Chapter 1). Spy comedy *Burn After Reading* placed Clooney among an ensemble of actors who collectively populate a complex structure of parallel and interweaving stories. Renown music photographer and video director Anton Corbijn directed *The American* based on the novel *A Very Private Gentleman*, author Martin Booth's existentialist tale of a gunsmith-to-the-assassins reflecting on the purpose of his profession as he quietly lives out his years in an Italian village. In comparison, *The Descendants* is a rather conventional 'dramedy' with Clooney playing a father working to hold his family together after his wife is seriously injured. For its source material, *Confessions of a Dangerous Mind* took the 'unauthorized biography' of Chuck Barris, a television game show creator, host and producer who claimed to have worked undercover for the CIA. Presented entirely in black and white, *Good Night, and Good Luck* focuses on the real-life confrontations between television journalist Edward R. Murrow and US Senator Joseph McCarthy during the latter's anti-Communist witch hunt (see Chapter 4). Clooney took only minor supporting on-screen roles in the latter two but they remain significant to his star brand as they became his first projects as director. *From Dusk Till Dawn* is the kind of film that might more usually be attributed to exploitation cinema, while *Burn After Reading, The American, Confessions of a Dangerous Mind,* and *Good Night, and Good Luck,* are too 'artsy' to be popular commercial propositions.

Clooney's positioning in the speciality sub-sector is not tied exclusively to the emergence of Indiewood though. He's appeared in other films that might be classed as specialized but which were financed and distributed by the main divisions of the majors. Apart from *Burn After Reading,* any of his films with the Coen Brothers (*O Brother, Where Art Thou?* (2000, Universal and Disney), *Intolerable*

Cruelty (2003, Universal) and *Hail, Caesar!* (2016, Universal), together with the sci-fi remake *Solaris* (2002, Fox), noirish period drama *The Good German* (2006, Warner Bros.) and political dramas *Syriana* (2005, Warner Bros.) and *The Ides of March* (2011, Columbia) are equally representative of speciality production.

Clooney's appearance in speciality films from the majors shows how divisions between popular and specialized cannot simply or directly be mapped onto a distinction between Hollywood against Indiewood or the independents. The bridging of Hollywood and Indiewood, while traversing the popular and speciality sectors, encapsulates the flexibility of Clooney's stardom. His involvements with Indiewood have seen his star brand acquire the image of independence but while firmly embedded within the core of Hollywood. The flexibility and mobility of Clooney's stardom therefore provides an exact point from which to appreciate the confusions and complex interweavings that exist between the multiple modes of production and distribution characterizing the industrial landscape of contemporary American film.

Post-studio stardom and star autonomy

Beyond the broad structures of the industry, a second way in which the independence/Hollywood dialectic works in flexible stardom is through the relationship of freelance elite actors to the Hollywood majors. As the making of individual star identities always involves coordination of multiple collective inputs, so the production of stardom is often referred to as a 'system', although stardom is perhaps best understood as a sub-system operating inside Hollywood's overall systems of production. Consequently, as the overall structure of the business changed, so the star sub-system has been transformed. During the 1930s and 1940s, some leading actors worked on an independent freelance basis (Carman 2016; Kemper

2010). Most actors holding star status were, however, employed on long-term exclusive contracts by the Hollywood majors. In this system, the majors moulded star careers, from nurturing raw acting talent to controlling the casting of and publicity for established names (McDonald 2000). As part of this system, actors hired the services of external talent agents, entertainment lawyers and maybe publicists to represent them in matters of employment, legal affairs and self-promotion. These inputs did not distract, however, from a general situation in which the production of stardom was largely concentrated among and internalized by the majors. Little or no space was left outside of Hollywood for actors to build the public exposure necessary for achieving stardom. With the majors controlling operations across the whole production-distribution-exhibition supply chain, and retaining stars exclusively under long-term contracts, the period was largely characterized by 'vertically integrated stardom' (McDonald 2013: 88–94).

In the years immediately following World War II, three factors challenged the Hollywood film industry: the decree from the Supreme Court ordering the majors to sell off their exhibition holdings, the rapid decline of the cinema-going audience, and the competition presented by the popularization of television. As part of measures to tackle these disruptions, the majors reduced risks and cut overhead costs by gradually releasing star talent from long-term contracts. Leading actors became part of a large freelance pool of creative talent available to the majors or independents for hiring on short-term single-project contracts. No longer salaried employees, freelance independent stars relied to an even greater extent on talent agents, personal managers, PR firms and entertainment attorneys to help broker their careers. By taking key functions in the production of stardom outside the majors, a network of service providers became leading players in the formation of a 'post-studio' star sub-system. It would be mistaken, however, to presume this resulted in the majors ceasing to play any significant part in the making of stardom.

The Hollywood oligopoly, represented by the handful of powerful companies in the US film industry who dominate distribution, has not disappeared or declined, but has rather has become strengthened through successive waves of conglomeration. Structurally, the American film business remains highly concentrated. This creates a bottleneck in the production of stardom, for, with few exceptions, only the major corporations of conglomerate Hollywood command the financial and operational resources to make, market and release films with the levels of mass global exposure necessary for generating and sustaining star visibility. In the post-studio sub-system, therefore, the majors still function as gatekeepers for stardom.

Clooney is a product of the post-studio star sub-system. As a freelance actor-for-hire, Clooney is an autonomous figure working for no single entity. Various parties from outside the majors have had a hand in steering his career, including representatives at the talent agencies William Morris and Creative Artists Agency, publicist Stan Rosenfield and lawyer Michael Adler. At the same time, since the mid-1990s Clooney's movie career has almost entirely been formed through films released, produced and/or financed by the majors or their Indiewood subsidiaries. Clooney's stardom exists, then, in conditions of dependent-independence vis-à-vis the majors: as an independent freelancer Clooney is not exclusively signed to any of the Hollywood majors yet his elite status is entirely dependent on the financial and corporate muscle flexed by the majors across domestic and international markets (McDonald 2013: 120–1). Clooney is then representative of the paradox at the heart of post-studio stardom: he is a free agent whose independence and star status is forever contingent on conglomerate Hollywood.

While Clooney emerges from the post-studio sub-system, part of the nostalgic aura that surrounds his star brand results from how his position in the industry harks back to the strong star-studio affiliations characteristic of the vertically integrated sub-system. Clooney has enjoyed the freedoms of star autonomy while at the same time building a long-term working relationship with a single company, Warner Bros. The television division built Clooney's fame with *ER*. Staying under the umbrella of the same corporate parentage, Clooney subsequently went on to work for Warner Bros. Pictures on *Batman & Robin* (1997), *Three Kings*, *The Perfect Storm*, all three episodes in the *Ocean's* trilogy (2001, 2004 and 2007), *Welcome to Collinwood* (2002), *Syriana, The Good German, Michael Clayton* (2007) and *Gravity* (2013). As discussed later, Warner also extended their talent relationship with Clooney by bankrolling his moves into 'independent' production with first-look deals for his companies Section Eight and Smokehouse. Consequently, Clooney appears as something of a throwback to vertically integrated stardom, with one corporation taking a central role in launching, growing and sustaining the star brand.

Like all stars, Clooney enjoys privileged status among the talent hierarchy of Hollywood, holding greater creative and economic power than most other actors. This power must be put in perspective, however. Stardom brings certain freedoms and privileges, but in conglomerate Hollywood, stars and their movies are only ever small elements – 'assets' or 'resources' – within massively extended corporate networks. When Clooney appeared for Universal Pictures in the 2003 release *Intolerable Cruelty*, he worked on a film from a division of Vivendi Universal, a French multinational with historical origins in water supply and waste management (Johnson and Orange 2004). Vivendi Universal had become one of the leading global media and communications conglomerates, with extensive international assets across television networks and channels, telecommunications, electronic games, music publishing and recording, and theme parks and resorts (Vivendi Universal SA 2003: 1–2). However, by the time he next worked for Universal on the 2008 release *Leatherheads*, the company was under new ownership having been acquired four years previously by General Electric, one of the world's largest companies diversified across aviation, energy, oil and gas, transportation, water, healthcare, and financial services (General Electric Company 2009:

4–10). Compared to many other creative workers, film stars most certainly enjoy far greater creative and financial freedoms, yet the consolidation of conglomerate Hollywood ensures star power is bounded and limited, operating only at a very localized level. Elite talent enjoys considerable creative decision-making authority in the production of individual film projects but this influence is contained within larger corporate structures where the control and direction of media operations is implemented through multiple tiers of management and governance. Immersed in the conditions of ownership structuring conglomerate Hollywood, Clooney is both star and subordinate; he may be a prized asset but, in the bigger picture, at the end of the day he is just an actor.

Clooney in the film market

Locating Clooney within the structures and systems of the industry provides a couple of perspectives on the flexibility of his stardom. A further way is offered by examining how Clooney's branded performances have been dispersed across the film marketplace. Stars are brands because they operate as signs of value, and just as Clooney has worked between different contexts of production, so the Clooney brand has occupied various positions in the film marketplace. To identify these, the following analysis employs four indices: production budgets, box office grosses, scale of release and film ratings. Respectively these represent the valuing, popularity, visibility and accessibility of the Clooney brand.

a) Budgets

Production budgets represent investment decisions. They are signs of the risk assumed by producers based on their anticipation of a film's likely commercial potential. While the fixing of budgets is never based purely on the contribution made by a star, for films that feature star names, in part budgets demonstrate judgments about the anticipated worth of a star brand. As such, budgets can be read as indicators of how producers *value* a star brand. Actual production budgets in Hollywood are matters of commercial confidentiality: closely guarded secrets that nobody outside the industry, and very few within the business itself, know with any certainty. Without any transparent disclosure of budgets, the information available is always incomplete, and so its accuracy must be treated with considerable caution. Not only do published numbers appear suspiciously neatly rounded (maybe $50 million and not, say, $52,136, 078) but also accountancy practices in Hollywood are notoriously and strategically complex, purposefully obfuscating the actual cost of a film (Daniels, Leedy and Sills 2006). Any citing of budgets must therefore always come with the caveat that these are 'reported' figures, i.e. numbers based on the best, or more usually the only, publicly available sources.

Reported budgets for Clooney's films up to mid-2016 are included in the Appendix. One sign of Clooney's flexible mobility is how these figures show him working on films crossing multiple tiers of production investment. Over the period discussed here, a measure of average budgets for Hollywood film was provided by annual figures published until 2007 by the Motion Picture Association of America (MPAA), the trade association representing the collective interests of the majors. When Clooney was establishing his movie stardom in the mid-to-late 1990s, the average annual cost of producing a film among MPAA members varied between $36.4 million and $51.5 million; from 2001 to 2007, the average cost ranged between $47.7 million and $70.8 million (see Appendix).[1] With reported budgets exceeding double or treble the MPAA average for the years in which they were produced, *Batman & Robin* (budget $125 million), *The Perfect Storm* ($140 million) and *Ocean's Twelve* (2004, $110 million) saw Clooney performing in films placed among

Commercial success can also be read as a measure of Clooney's standing among Hollywood's star elite. Annually, from 1932 to 2013, the Quigley Publishing Company asked US film exhibitors to rank the actors whom they regarded as the top money-making stars. As such the poll gave some measure of how industry practitioners yearly viewed the market value for stars. In the years when *The Perfect Storm* and *Ocean's Eleven* were released, Clooney respectively ranked 3rd and 2nd in the poll (Quigley 2014) (Table 3.1). For other years it is difficult if not impossible to see any co-relation between Clooney's ranking and any single hit. His 6th position in 2005 most probably came from a combination of the $18.5 million grossed by *Ocean's Twelve* once it continued its run after opening late the previous year, plus the $38.9 million (of an eventual $50.8 million total) *Syriana* grossed by year end after opening in November (figures from D'Alessandro 2006). Similarly, Clooney's 3rd-place ranking for 2007 was likely based on the $117.2 million grossed by *Ocean's Thirteen* plus the $39.2 million *Michael Clayton* accrued by the end of the year (figures from *Variety* 2008). With those two films pulling in a combined total of $156.4 million, Clooney was placed in the 2007 rankings behind Johnny Depp and Will Smith who had respectively starred that year in *Pirates of the Caribbean: At the World's End* (domestic gross $309.4 million) and *I Am Legend* (domestic gross $206.1 million). As Clooney ranked above 4th-placed Matt Damon, star of the $227.5 million grossing *The Bourne Ultimatum*, the third part in a series for which the first two instalments had already grossed $297.9 million domestically, it might be reasonable to presume the rankings were based on *perceptions* of box office value rather than any actual calculation. The same could be said of Clooney's rankings over subsequent years, when despite his films achieving relatively low grosses, he still ranked 5th (2006), 8th (2008), 4th (2009), 9th (2010) and 2nd (2011) (Quigley 2014). Even when box office data contradicted Clooney's rankings in these years, respondents to the Quigley poll still judged him among the highest money-making stars.

Table 3.1 Annual Star Rankings, Box Office Grosses and Rankings (2000–11)[a]

Year	Quigley Ranking Top Money-Making Stars	Films Released in Calendar Year	Total North American Gross $m	Film's Annual Box Office Ranking
2000	3	*The Perfect Storm*	182.6	4
		O Brother, Where Art Thou?	45.5	56[b]
2001	2	*Ocean's Eleven*	183.4	8[b]
2005	6	*Good Night, and Good Luck*	31.6	89[b]
		Syriana	50.8	56[b]
2006	5	*The Good German*	1.3	229[b]
2007	3	*Michael Clayton*	49.0	45[b]
		Ocean's Thirteen	117.2	26
2008	8	*Leatherheads*	31.4	95
		Burn After Reading	60.4	52
2009	4	*Up in the Air*	83.8	38[b]
		The Men Who Stare at Goats	32.4	87[b]
		Fantastic Mr. Fox	21.0	107[b]
2010	9	*The American*	35.6	84
2011	2	*The Ides of March*	41.0	74[b]
		The Descendants	82.6	39[b]

Sources: author's analysis of data compiled from Quigley (2014) and www.boxofficemojo.com

Notes

[a] This analysis cross-refers the years Clooney appeared in the annual Quigley poll of top money-making stars with the North American grosses and annual box office rankings for his films released in those years.
[b] Films with runs extending across two years. Ranking is based on where the eventual total gross would place the film if it had completed the run in the year of release.

c) Scale of release

Box office gross alone gives a misleading measure of a film's position in the marketplace, for films do not enter the market on equal terms. If box office gross gives some indication of a film's popularity, differences in the scale of release, measured by the total number of screens a film shows on at its Widest Point of Release (WPR), determines the public availability or *visibility* of any film and, where relevant, its star. Furthermore, the scale of release also provides another measure of how a star brand is valued, for just as producers must make budget decisions about production investment, so distributors have had to assess the total number of celluloid and now digital prints necessary to optimize a film's performance in theatrical exhibition.[4] Economic efficiency demands this calculation must be based on some estimate of the likely size of cinema-going audience for a film, and so WPR can be read as an index of how a distributor intended to position a film according to presumptions about the anticipated audience.

Scale of release, measured by WPR, will inevitably enable or restrict a film's capacity for earning box office revenues. The positioning of any film in the market must therefore be seen through the correlation of box office (popularity) and WPR (visibility). Figure 3.2 plots total box office gross against WPR for the North American releases of all films in which Clooney appeared in a lead or off-lead role by mid-2016. While it is possible to pick out the positions of individual films, the main purpose of this analysis is to identify patterns of clustering, i.e. close groupings of films according to common levels of popularity and visibility. In Clooney's case, two particular clusters can be discerned. Positioned at the upper right corner of the scattergraph are films that achieved both high grosses and wide releases – i.e. *The Perfect Storm, Batman & Robin* and the *Ocean's* trilogy – with domestic grosses each surpassing $130 million and WPRs exceeding 3,000 screens. As the graph shows, these few 'hits' are unrepresentative of Clooney's more general positioning in the market. Clooney has more commonly occupied a middling position, falling outside the hit-driven market but rarely declining into commercial failure. This is the space occupied by those films described earlier as medium- or lower-budget productions. Among medium-budget productions, the scale of release ranged from 1,775 screens (*Syriana*) to 2,798 screens

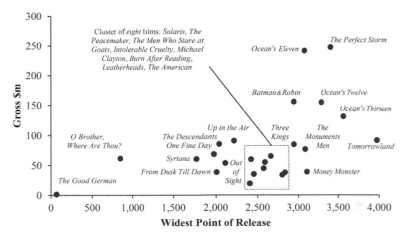

Figure 3.2 North American Grosses and Scale of Release (1996–2016). [1]

Source: author's analysis of data at www.boxofficemojo.com.

Note

[1]Chart plots popularity against visibility by cross-referencing total box office gross against widest point of release in North America. Analysis is confined to the 25 films released between 1996 and 2016 in which Clooney took lead or off-lead roles (see note for figure 3.1). Grosses are inflation adjusted to 2013 prices.

(*Leatherheads*), while releases for lower-budget productions extended from the 2,007 or 2,038 screens that *From Dusk Till Dawn* and *The Descendants* opened on, to the 2,657 and 2,833 screens for *Burn After Reading* and *The American*. As many films distributed theatrically in North America struggle to appear on more than just a handful of screens, these cases must be regarded as major releases, and at the upper end here, films received a scale of release nearing that of the hits. With these films, however, extensive visibility did not correspond to high-grossing popularity, for films occupying this position ranged from the $19.4 million grossed by *Solaris* (2,406 screens) to the $85.5 million and $91 million of *The Descendants* (2,038 screens) and *Up in the Air* (2,218 screens).

Clooney's market positioning has therefore seen him moving between big-budget, widely released, high-grossing hits,

Mirador a two-year exclusive deal to produce television series and TV movies, although ultimately no actual output emerged from the arrangement. Complementing the television work of Mirador, Clooney also formed Left Bank Productions as a film production outfit, agreeing a three-year first-look development and production deal in November 1996 with Warner Bros., and the following August the company was renamed Maysville after the Clooney family's home town (Johnson 1996a and 1996b). Maysville also looked towards producing for television, signing a pair of two-year development deals with Warner Bros. TV and CBS, creating an arrangement whereby Maysville made series for the former and TV movies for the latter (Hontz 1998). To run this second company, Clooney partnered with Robert Lawrence, who had recently produced *Die Hard with a Vengeance* (1995) and *Clueless* (1995). Maysville announced a slate of twelve films, half with Clooney to star. Lawrence said the company was committed to 'looking for thinking-man's, character-driven action-thrillers' (quoted in Karon 1997a: 1). Among prospective film projects with Clooney's name attached were the romcom *A Thousand Kisses*, political thriller *Designated Survivor*, prison drama *The Castle*, Gulag escape tale *The Long Walk*, and espionage drama *The Catcher Was a Spy* (Busch 1997c; Cox and Fleming 1999; Galloway 1998; Hindes 1998; Karon 1997b). *Kilroy*, a one-off inside Hollywood realistic television comedy, was also planned, with Clooney co-writing and executive-producing (Hontz 1999: 1). None of these projects, however, came to fruition, and as the three-year film deal with Warner neared its end, in September 1999 Clooney parted from Lawrence (Petrikin 1999).

Following the split, Maysville made the television movie *Fail Safe* (2000) with Clooney playing a supporting role while taking an executive-producer credit. Following events after a communication blunder launches a nuclear attack against Moscow, *Fail Safe* was a remake of the 1964 Cold War film drama of the same name produced by Columbia. Foregrounding the madness of mutually assured destruction, *Fail Safe* gives an early on-screen illustration of the liberal sentiments that gradually inflected the Clooney brand (see Chapter 4). Broadcast live on CBS, *Fail Safe* mirrored the periodicity of the dramatic context by nostalgically paying homage to the production techniques of a former media age. With this self-conscious recreation of political and media pasts, *Fail Safe* showed Clooney using his independent company as a vehicle for exercising creative autonomy. More conventionally, Mayville also remained a production participant in *Rock Star* (2001), a project developed as *Metal God* before the company's dissolution, with Lawrence as producer and Clooney as executive producer (Fleming 1999c).

Mirador and Maysville were almost entirely unproductive, and Clooney's move into independent production only really took off with Section Eight, the company he formed with Steven Soderbergh, Clooney's director on *Out of Sight* (1998) (see Chapter 1). Section Eight was set up at Warner in December 1999, further consolidating the link between Clooney and the major (Kit 1999b). To steer the company, executives with experience of working for the majors were appointed to senior positions. Ben Cosgove, former director of creative affairs at TriStar Pictures and previously senior VP of production at Maysville, was immediately appointed as president for Section Eight, and in June 2001 he was joined by co-president Jennifer Fox, Vice President of Production at Universal and a producer on Soderbergh's *Erin Brockovich* (2000) (Kit 2001). Actor Grant Heslov, a personal friend of Clooney's, was appointed director of development. One of the declared aims of Section Eight was to provide a launch pad for new directors (McLean 2006: A2). In practice, however, very few first-time directors (i.e. Gregory Jacobs, and Anthony and Joe Russo) got a break from Section Eight. A third of the company's films were directed by Soderbergh, two by Clooney, and others from names with established directing credits, including Christopher Nolan, Todd Haynes, John Maybury, Richard Linklater and Tony Gilroy. Signing a new three-year non-exclusive first-look deal in September 2001 preserved the Warner link and Section Eight moved into the old office of Jack Warner. According to Clooney, the decision to continue was made in part due to his strong professional relationship with Warner's head of worldwide production, Lorenzo di Bonaventura (Fleming 2001). Although Section Eight was sponsored by Warner, the two parties agreed the sindie would keep overheads low in return for Warner making minimal intervention in the company's operations (McClintock 2005). That independence was compromised on at least one occasion, however, when Warner Bros. sacked director Ted Griffin on the comedy *Rumor Has It …* (2005) (Holson 2005). Signing a two-year first-look deal in July 2003 with Warner Bros. Television, the company diversified with the formation of Section Eight Television (Warner Bros. 2003), subsequently producing the miniseries *K Street* (2003) and *Unscripted* (2005).

Sindiependence provides a further perspective on how Clooney's stardom flexibly traverses popular and speciality sectors of the industry and market. In January 2000, with the company still to be named, Section Eight announced its first project would be *Ocean's Eleven* (see Chapter 2). Remake rights had been acquired by producer Jerry Weintraub, who was based at Warner Bros., where di Bonaventura got the studio to agree to support the production with Clooney confirmed to star and Soderbergh to direct (Moerk 2000). From the start, the project was aimed at the hit market. Various high-profile names were rumoured to be joining the cast, including Bruce Willis, Johnny Depp, Mike Myers, Mark Wahlberg, Ralph Fiennes, Luke and Owen Wilson, and Joel and Ethan Coen (Brodesser 2000; Fleming 2000a: 1, 2000b and 2000c: 7). Eventually Clooney fronted a core ensemble featuring actors who were star names in their own right, including Julia Roberts, Brad Pitt and Matt Damon. As discussed earlier, the film was budgeted and given a scale of release to create a hit. After grossing over $450 million worldwide, Warner readily stepped up to fund two further instalments in the trilogy. Commercial success made the *Ocean's* films the most visible

manifestation of Section Eight but they were uncharacteristic of
the company's output. More commonly, the company made lower-
budgeted productions pitched at the speciality market, including
Far From Heaven (2002), director Todd Haynes's homage to 1950s
melodrama, con artist crime comedy *Criminal* (2004) (a remake
of the Argentine *Nueve reinas* (2000)), and Richard Linklater's
animated adaptation of the Philip K. Dick sci-fi novel *A Scanner
Darkly* (2006). As the company's star asset, Clooney's on-screen
stardom was deployed by Section Eight across the market spectrum,
from the popular *Ocean's* movies, to the speciality niche products
*Welcome to Collinwood, Confessions of a Dangerous Mind, Good Night,
and Good Luck, The Good German* and *Michael Clayton.*

Among Clooney's output, sindiependent production has
combined with narrative content, aesthetic choices, marketing
communications, and Indiewood releasing to position a film and the
star in the speciality market. A good example of this convergence is
The Good German. Based on the book by Joseph Kanon, the narrative
tells a tale of romance and deceit set among Cold War tensions in
the ruins of Berlin immediately after the conclusion of World War
II. Director Soderbergh intentionally set out to evoke classical
Hollywood, employing obsolete production technologies from the
1940s and adopting a black and white visual style. The nostalgia
also carried over to the film's marketing with posters imitating
the artwork used to sell *Casablanca* (1942) (Gallagher 2013: 79)
(Figure 3.4). While evoking the glamour of a former Hollywood
era, *The Good German* also nodded towards documentary realism
through the inclusion of archival newsreel footage. Despite evoking
the filmic past, at the same time *The Good German* departed from
faithful pastiche by including forms of profanity and representations
of sex or violence that would have been impossible when Hollywood
was still regulated by the Production Code. Not only in its look
but also its complex plotting, morally ambiguous characters, and
portrayal of the American and Soviet military as gangs occupying a

any film to become a 'hit' even in the modest terms of the speciality market. By the time the domestic run ended in mid-April, *The Good German* had grossed only $1.3 million, and similarly took a poor $4.6 million internationally. With *The Good German*, artistic ambition exceeded commercial attraction. Despite being a critical and commercial failure, *The Good German* still added to the Clooney brand, for with its pastiche stylings and appeals to retro cinephilic taste, the film enhanced the nostalgic aura and artistic gloss of his stardom.

Working with Soderbergh is important to the Clooney brand in more ways than just the running of Section Eight. As noted in Chapter 1, Soderbergh's direction of *Out of Sight* stabilized and defined the Clooney brand, and subsequently the two worked together on the *Ocean's* trilogy and *Solaris*. After Soderbergh's first feature *sex, lies, and videotape* (1989) attracted critical and commercial success, winning the Palme d'Or at the Cannes Film Festival and achieving a $24.7 million domestic gross on a production budget of $1.2 million, Soderbergh became the poster boy of contemporary American independent cinema.[6] With their respective creative identifies, Clooney and Soderbergh mutually inflected their respective brands: just as working with Clooney on *Out of Sight* and the *Ocean's* films marked the 'emerging popular Soderbergh' (Gallagher 2013: 150), so the association with Soderbergh on *Solaris*, *The Good German* and Section Eight's more unconventional productions contributed to the emergence of the 'indie' or 'specialized' Clooney.

In November 2005, it was announced Section Eight was to disband, reportedly because Soderbergh wanted to focus on directing and Clooney on acting and directing (McClintock 2005). Over the six and a half years the company was active, Section Eight produced three outright hits with the *Ocean's* series. *Syriana* and *Michael Clayton* performed respectably at the box office, but *The Good German, Welcome to Collinwood* (grossing $336,620 worldwide on a $10 million budget) and *Criminal* ($929,233 worldwide, budget unknown) were commercial flops. Closure of Section Eight in August 2006 coincided with the announcement that Clooney was moving on to partner with Heslov in forming a new company, Smoke House (with a logo reading Smokehouse), agreeing a three-year first-look production and development deal with Warner Bros.' film and television divisions (Kit 2006). When that deal expired, Smoke House broke from Warner, signing an exclusive two-year first-look deal with Sony to develop and produce films (Sony Pictures 2009). Coming at a time when the major was cutting back on production deals, Amy Pascal, co-chair of Sony Picture Entertainment, justified the move, saying 'we see real value in opening our doors to producers with their critical and commercial track record and their artistic point of view' (quoted in Graser 2009: 1). In June 2014, the relationship expanded to a two-year deal with Sony Pictures Television to produce comedy and drama series for broadcast, cable and digital (Goldberg 2014).

Stars are known for their acting but flexible stardom has generated a space in which elite actors have extended their contributions to other elements of the film-making process. Working through his independent outfits, Clooney has enlarged the scope of his creative roles in three directions. After *Confessions of a Dangerous Mind* and *Good Night, and Good Luck*, his directing career continued with half the episodes of *Unscripted* for Section Eight, and with *Leatherheads*, *The Ides of March* and *The Monuments Men* (2014) for Smoke House. Secondly, with Heslov, Clooney co-wrote *Good Night, and Good Luck*, *The Ides of March* and *The Monuments Men*.[7] Finally, after Maysville's *Fail Safe* and *Rock Star*, through his subsequent companies Clooney acquired a roster of executive-producer or producer credits. It can be ambiguous what exact responsibilities lay behind such credits. According to definitions applied by the Producers Guild of America (PGA), an executive producer 'supervises, either on his/her own authority (entrepreneur executive producer) or subject to the authority of an employer (employee executive producer) one or more producers in the performance of all of his/her/their producer functions on single or multiple productions'. A producer, however, 'initiates, coordinates, supervises and controls, either on his/her own authority, or subject to the authority of an employer, all aspects of the motion-picture and/or television production process, including creative, financial, technological and administrative', and 'is involved throughout all phases of production from inception to completion' (PGA n.d.). Across both categories, Clooney's producing credits have included some of the films he's acted in (e.g. *Welcome to Collinwood, Syriana, Michael Clayton* and *The American*) but also films where he has no on-screen role (e.g. *Far From Heaven* and *A Scanner Darkly*). With Smoke House, however, Clooney took a producer credit on films including the true-life hostage thriller *Argo* (2012), bittersweet family tale *August: Osage County* (2013) and political-comedy-drama *Our Brand is Crisis* (2015). As an actor-director-producer-writer, Clooney has joined the Hollywood hyphenates: individuals who operate across multiple creative functions in the film-making process. These multifaceted figures are not a new development: decades before, Charlie Chaplin, Ida Lupino and Orson Welles, for example, proliferated their creative responsibilities. Even so, in the vertically integrated sub-system, the contribution of stars was generally neatly bounded by a highly compartmentalized division of labour. With the post-studio star sub-system, however, multifunctional status is now commonplace. Clooney is therefore a figure illustrative of a context in which flexible stardom has made multifunctionality 'the new normal' (Feeney 2013).

Conclusion

Flexible stardom multiplies and spreads a star's presences, configuring the independence/Hollywood dialectic in multiple ways.

Clooney is an independent freelance actor but his star status remains dependent on the majors. He flexibly moves across different models of production or distribution, occupying various positions in the film market. Clooney has appeared in high-budget, wide-releasing event movie productions, but more frequently in forms of specialized production from the majors and their subsidiaries. Sindiependence has taken Clooney's stardom in other directions. As a principal executive for his own company, Clooney has moved beyond creative labour and into management. Through Section Eight and Smoke House, his influence extends up the decision-making ladder to taking an active role in selecting, developing and steering films through production. Running a sindie, while proliferating his roles to become an acting-directing-producing-writing hyphenate, Clooney has gained the creative freedom to make films that otherwise may not have been made by the majors, even if those opportunities have only been made possible by receiving financial input from the majors.

When considering the workings of the post-studio star sub-system in conglomerate Hollywood, it is necessary to look beyond the on-screen appearances of stars and to note the many other presences they have through the full range of roles or functions they perform both inside and outside the movie industry. Compared to the upfront hyper-visibility of the actor-star, the work of the writer, executive producer or producer is hidden and anonymous. Rather than consider these roles as existing outside of or apart from the star brand, it is important to recognize these various creative and business functions as brand extensions, actions that expand and grow the reach of the star brand (McDonald 2013: 58–9). While Clooney's roles as director, writer or producer are not immediately perceptible in the same way as his acting, they still feature in the dispersal of the Clooney brand. Once the multiplication of these contributions is assessed in total, it might be argued that it becomes misleading to describe someone like Clooney as a 'star', for such a label seemingly limits understanding of his place in the industry to the role of actor alone. Possibly so, yet on the other hand it must be recognized that it is only by his status as an elite branded star-actor that Clooney has been able to traverse the industry and occupy the range of roles he has. Post-studio flexible stardom may pull the actor-star in many different directions, although the performed brand continues to centre and anchor the star's movement within the industrial space of Hollywood.

Notes

1 MPAA reporting published these figures as the average 'negative cost', i.e. the average cost of producing a finished film negative. Negative cost combines production expenditure with studio overheads and capitalized interest. As the MPAA stopped publishing this data after 2007, average figures for subsequent years are unavailable.
2 As noted in the endnotes to Chapter 2, however, in *Gravity* Clooney played only a secondary, supporting role to Sandra Bullock.
3 Based on North American grosses at the end of the respective calendar years.
4 Before the conversion to digital cinema exhibition, $1,500 to $2,000 was commonly cited as the typical price range for reproducing a celluloid release print of a feature film (see Tyson, J. n.d.).
5 CARA defines these ratings in the following terms. PG advises 'Parents [are] urged to give "parental guidance." May contain some material parents might not like for their young children.' PG-13 is applied where 'Parents are urged to be cautious. Some material maybe inappropriate for pre-teenagers.' R requires anyone under the age of 17 to be accompanied by a parent or adult guardian and warns a film 'Contains some adult material. Parents are urged to learn more about the film before taking their young children with them' (CARA n.d.a).
6 This was despite Universal handling the releasing of Soderbergh's subsequent five features, either through the major's main distribution division or by the speciality subsidiary Gramercy Pictures (a joint venture with would-be European major PolyGram Filmed Entertainment).
7 *The Ides of March* adapts the 2008 stage drama *Farragut North* from playwright and screenwriter Beau Willimon, who worked with Clooney and Heslov on the screenplay.

4 ACTORVIST STARDOM: ENTERTAINMENT/ POLITICS

Intersections between entertainment and politics have strongly inflected the Clooney brand. On-screen, Clooney has acted in, and sometimes directed, written or produced, film and television work with overt political content. Off-screen, he's developed an alternative mediated identity, speaking out about various matters of political contention: labour union policy in the entertainment business, the Iraq War, gay rights, the influence of big money in political party campaigning, and humanitarian disaster and genocide. Part actor, part activist, the label 'actorvist' suitably describes how Clooney has become both a film and a political 'performer'. Unlike other Hollywood names such as Ronald Reagan and Arnold Schwarzenegger, Clooney has not entered formal governmental administration. Instead his off-screen engagements with politics have taken the form of an 'entertainer who pronounces on politics and claims the right to represent peoples and causes, but does so without seeking or acquiring elected office … [making] public gestures or statements aimed at changing specific public policy decisions' (Street 2004: 438). Clooney has a long-term relationship with politics. In newspaper and magazine profiles, Clooney has repeatedly told stories of how, since his childhood, his broadcast journalist father Nick provided him with a politically principled role model. 'I think if you're the son of an anchorman,' Clooney has said, 'you're involved in politics. That is part of what you do, and so we were always socially active and always socially involved and politically involved' (quoted in Daunt 2007a: E5).

When movie stars engage with politics a reciprocal exchange of meanings takes place: political positions inflect the star brand while stardom becomes a prism through which politics are filtered, communicated and given significance. In Clooney's case, the politics of his brand arises from his emergence as a star of the liberal Left. 'I'm an old-time liberal and I don't apologise for it,' he's proudly stated (quoted in Harris 2005). Kicking back at conservative stigmatization of liberals, in March 2006 Clooney published a piece in *The Huffington Post* titled 'I am a Liberal. There, I Said It!'[1]

Too many people run away from the label. They whisper it like you'd whisper 'I'm a Nazi.' Like it's a dirty word. But turn away from saying 'I'm a liberal' and it's like you're turning away from saying that blacks should be allowed to sit in the front of the bus, that women should be able to vote and get paid the same as a man, that McCarthy was wrong, that Vietnam was a mistake.

(Joyner 2006)

Alignment with the Left in part contributes to the nostalgic aura of the Clooney brand, not because he looks backwards to a political past – on the contrary, he consistently engages with present-day issues – but rather through how his political positioning places him in the tradition of other Hollywood actors who have outwardly communicated Leftist positions through their on- and off-screen identities. Alongside Susan Sarandon, Tim Robbins and Sean Penn, Clooney is a modern member of the Hollywood Left, a lineage stretching back through American film history with high-profile figures including Robert Redford, Jane Fonda, Warren Beatty, Barbra Streisand, Paul Newman, Gregory Peck, Humphrey Bogart, Katharine Hepburn, Harry Belafonte, Edward G. Robinson and Charles Chaplin (Ross 2011).

This chapter examines the mediation of politics by the Clooney brand. Initially examining Clooney's on-screen politics, analyses of *Three Kings* (1999) and *Syriana* (2005) consider how the narrative positioning of Clooney's characters articulate but also contradict or weaken the political critique in these films. The chapter then turns to Clooney's off-screen politics. As figures with established public profiles, film stars can magnify public awareness of political issues. Yet when Hollywood stars openly voice political positions it exposes them to partisan criticism and potential ridicule. Clooney has attracted both. Foundational here is a crisis of legitimacy, questioning on what basis privileged figures from the sphere of entertainment can represent the disadvantaged or authoritatively claim knowledge of matters in the sphere of politics. The chapter sees how Clooney has tackled the issue of political legitimization by constructing a self-reflexive critique of stars as the magnifiers of politics. It examines how Clooney has negotiated the contradictions of politicized stardom as he's become a target for, and responded to, conservative criticisms of liberal Hollywood. Remaining sections then deal with Clooney's interventions in three areas of political contention: entertainment industry labour disputes, Hollywood fundraising for electioneering, and humanitarian campaigning.

On-screen politics and the liberal conscience

Politics play a central part in a body of Clooney's film and television work. Party politics provide the setting for *The Ides of March* (2011), directed, co-written and acted in by Clooney, but also the improvised miniseries *K Street* (2003), co-produced by Clooney and Steven Soderbergh through the television arm of their Section Eight production company. With *Michael Clayton* (2007) and *Money Monster* (2016), corporate malfeasance is seen to be a consequence of capitalism. This critique is limited, however, for in their respective ways the two films are restricted to identifying and uncovering a single rogue entity responsible for wrongdoing. As one reviewer of *Money Monster* noted, the 'implication is that, once this one rotten apple is removed, the rest of the barrel will be fine' (Alleva 2016: 20). For *The Good German* (2006) (see Chapter 3) and the comedies *Confessions of a Dangerous Mind* (2002) and *Hail, Caesar!* (2016), the Cold War provides a mere backdrop, but the political tensions of the period gain more significant treatment in *Fail Safe* (2000) and *Good Night, and Good Luck* (2005). With the latter, Clooney co-wrote, directed and took a supporting role in this dramatization of the processes of television news production leading to the famous 1954 on-air criticism delivered by broadcast journalist Edward R. Murrow against Senator Joseph McCarthy's anti-Communist witch hunt (pmw8000 2011). Beyond this historically specific case, the larger issue of the film is with the responsibilities of news media 'speaking truth to power'. This preoccupation with articulating truth extends to the narrative and aesthetic construction of the film: not only does the story involve real-life historical figures and incidents but the look and sound of the film work towards veracity and authenticity by adopting an artful black and white visual style faithful to television production of the 1950s, accompanied by new recordings of music standards from the period. On *Good Night, and Good Luck*, writer-director-actor Clooney likened the work of the film-makers to that of journalists: 'Because we were dealing with people whose life goal was to focus on accuracy, it meant that we couldn't misrepresent. We had to be extraordinarily careful with the facts. We treated everything like journalists: every scene in the movie we double sourced' (quoted in Kaufman 2005). *Good Night, and Good Luck* is grounded in a historically specific moment but, at the time the film was released in 2005, it was widely viewed as an allegory for contemporary anxieties. Apart from a general concern with how commercialization of the media shapes the news agenda with deleterious effects on journalistic values, the film resonated in the post-9/11 climate as opportunistic exploitation of fears over alleged menaces from outside and inside the US stifled political debate and civil liberties. For *Rolling Stone*, Peter Travers (2005) observed, 'Clooney has crafted a period piece that speaks potently to a here-and-now when constitutional rights are being threatened in the name of the Patriot Act, and the American media trade in truth for access'. With its reflections on the responsibilities of political journalism, *Good Night, and Good Luck* belongs to a body of output in Clooney's career concerned with the politics of media communication. *K Street* and *The Ides of March* dealt with the roles of lobbyists and campaign managers in shaping the presentation of party politics, and *Money Monster* satirized how television creates and distorts public knowledge of financial markets. By implicitly or explicitly questioning the role of mediated communication as an active force for shaping public consciousness, this output has variously offered meta-reflections on the media as a sphere for the production and performance of political discourse.

This interrogation of the role which the media play in shaping political discourse must be turned back onto Clooney's own output and the role of star performance in enacting politics: how have Clooney's own films and his star brand mediated political content? *Three Kings* and *Syriana* are useful examples to consider in this context, with both deploying Clooney's on-screen presence in cynical reflections on the consequences of petroleum politics for US foreign policy in the Middle East. Set in March 1991 immediately following the conclusion of the Persian Gulf War and Operation Desert Storm, *Three Kings* is an anti-war action-adventure black comedy allegorizing and satirizing US intervention in the Middle East. Specifically, the film criticizes how the government of President George H. W. Bush betrayed the uprising against Saddam Hussein by Iraqi insurgents. Originally, the role of Special Forces officer Archie Gates was written for Clint Eastwood, but when he, Mel Gibson and Nicolas Cage all declined, Clooney directly appealed to director David O. Russell for the part. Gates/Clooney leads a small group of army reservists who embark on an unauthorized mission to uncover gold bullion stolen from Kuwait by Saddam's military forces. This is no noble quest: the group are selfishly motivated, coveting the gold for personal gain rather than returning war plunder to its rightful owner. Quickly, however, the search becomes a political and moral odyssey, for the journey exposes the group to the deceit and duplicity of US intervention in the region. Despite the avowed aim of liberating Kuwait from the Iraqi invasion, the film sees the deployment of troops by Western powers as principally aimed at protecting oil supplies. This gold heist adventure therefore becomes a metaphor for the extraction of wealth by the US from the region. While the film links petroleum geopolitics to international conflict, this critique is subordinated to a narrative of humanitarian crisis. After the Gulf War concluded, various factions, encouraged by the promise of US support from the Bush government, rebelled in the hope of toppling Saddam's regime. When coalition forces failed to advance into Iraq, and the ceasefire agreement preserved Saddam's power, however, the insurgency was viciously quashed. This situation is replayed in *Three Kings* as Gates/Clooney and his men witness the persecution of rebel villagers by Saddam's troops. In response Gates/Clooney and his men forego their claim on the gold in favour of helping the villagers to safety across the border with Iran.

Focusing on a socially diverse male group fighting and outwitting an evil enemy, *Three Kings* follows many conventions of the combat movie. With its jaundiced take on US diplomacy, the film applies post-Vietnam cynicism to another overseas conflict: there is no honour in war and the men involved have little understanding of, or enthusiasm for, the fight. The meaninglessness of the situation is underscored by the film's absurdist tone, with bizarre incidents turning the film into an 'exercise in popular but palpable surrealism' (Schickel 1999: 93): for example, the map indicating the location of the gold is found in the anus of a captured Iraqi soldier, and a cow explodes after stepping on a landmine. Situated among the mayhem, Gates/Clooney voices an overall sense of disillusionment about the war when he says to his superior, Colonel Ron Horn (Mykelti Williamson), 'I don't even know what we did here.' Once the hunt for the gold commences, Gates/Clooney becomes the central moral conscience of the film. Witnessing the fate of villagers at the hands of Saddam's men, Gates/Clooney articulates the film's central critique: 'Bush told the people to rise up against Saddam. They thought they'd have our support. They don't. Now they're getting slaughtered.' Clooney signed up to do *Three Kings* in July 1998, before its release in October 1999. Work on the film therefore overlapped with the period in which Clooney's final season on *ER* was produced and aired. In one respect, Gates stands at a major remove from Dr Doug Ross, a taker rather than a saver of lives. At the same time, Gates and Ross bear many similarities. Although working in highly regulated and disciplined institutional contexts, both break the rules, rejecting the commands of their superiors to achieve principled ends. Just as Ross protected children against the abuses of familial rule, so Gates becomes the carer and guardian of a people against the abuses of Saddam's dictatorship. Gates was therefore consistent with the pre-constituted meanings of the Clooney brand.

Depicting a war and story with obvious racial divisions, the producers behind *Three Kings* set out to carefully manage representations of race. Prior to production, Warner Bros.' legal department invited US academic Jack G. Shaheen, renowned for his studies of Arab representation in American film and television, to read and recommend changes to the script. Shaheen became a consultant for the film after producer Charles Roven requested his assistance in 'helping us portray the Iraqi characters as more fully developed characters and making sure, whenever possible, that we stay away from uncomfortable stereotypes' (quoted in Shaheen 2009: 520). Eschewing simple stereotypes, the film includes some Iraqi characters of depth and complexity, most notably the Republican Guard torturer Captain Said, and the leader of the rebels Amir Abdulah. However, casting French-Moroccan Said Taghmaoul and

New Zealand Maori Cliff Curtis in these roles distracts from this intention, for it seems Iraqis can be played by anyone but themselves. *Three Kings* received positive endorsements from representatives of the Arab-American and Muslim communities. Speaking as president of the American-Arab Anti-Discrimination Committee, Hala Maksoud said the film 'shows the Arab and the Muslim and their complexity, with feelings and normal aspirations ... We're happy that for once, we are not stereotyped by Hollywood' (quoted in Finnigan 1999: 6). Salam Al-Marayati of the Muslim Public Affairs Council said: 'For the first time on screen, you see the human face of the Iraqi people' (ibid. 36). Despite these validations, *Three Kings* can be seen to fall back on simplified types. Following conventions commonly used to represent the enemy in combat films, Iraqi troops – the largest proportion of Iraqi figures seen in the film – are portrayed as cowardly, easily duped, and seemingly unable to dodge flying bullets, or in the absurdist play of the film, an exploding football. Similarly, with the exception of Abdulah/Curtis, the escaping rebel villagers are an identityless mass, shepherded to safety by their idiosyncratically individualized American guardians.

This backdrop reflects on Clooney's positioning in the racial politics of *Three Kings*. Leading the exodus of the oppressed, Gates/ Clooney takes a people, although they are not his people, to a 'promised land'. Gates/Clooney emerges as the 'white saviour' or 'white messiah', a figure occasionally found in Hollywood film who is

an alienated hero, a misfit within his own society, mocked and rejected until he becomes a leader of a minority group or of foreigners. He finds himself by self-sacrifice to liberate the natives ... Often the white outsider is instantly worshipped by the natives, treated like visiting royalty or a god ... The messiah is marked by charisma, the extraordinary quality that legitimizes his role as leader and that of the foreign population as followers.

(Vera and Gordon 2003: 33–4)

While overtly critical of the actions and motivations of US intervention in the Middle East, Gates's story equally supports the case for American intervention and the supremacy of white leadership: 'despite its acid critique of American foreign policy in the Gulf War and its persistent black humor, the film is at heart a sentimental story about an American good guy standing up to absolute evil ... giving up the gold and risking his life to save Iraqi refugees' (ibid. 50). As the Iraqi insurgents are only rescued through the actions of a small bunch of American heroes, US intervention is validated as a necessary condition for achieving a final state of peace, security and freedom. As one reviewer noted: 'What we have here is an anti-war film that wants it both ways. It shows the horror of war, but then says Americans should help wage a war against Saddam, as though that wouldn't produce the same kind of harrowing stories about dead kids and wives that the film shows us' (Landesman 2000: 9). In the end the film appears to call 'for American imperialism to be moralized rather than rejected' (Davies 2005: 408). The film rejects 'bad' intervention, perpetrated to secure oil supplies, only to then support benevolent intervention. Ultimately, *Three Kings* therefore affirms rather than challenges the authority of the US to act as the 'World's policeman'.

Developed and produced in the years immediately following the terrorist attacks of 11 September 2001, and during a time when the ensuing US occupations of Afghanistan and Iraq were still active, *Syriana* presented a timely questioning of petroleum politics in the formation of US policy for the Middle East and its catalysing effect on Islamic fundamentalism. Rooting its arguments in real world politics, *Syriana* belongs to a body of films informed by the insights of retired Central Intelligence Agency (CIA) officers (Jenkins 2012: 115–32). Drawing on the memoirs of former CIA operative Robert Baer (2002), some of the narrative elements in *Syriana* share similarities with Baer's own experiences of working in the Middle East and his eventual disillusionment with, and rejection by, the Agency. Baer acted as advisor to the film, sometimes assisting director and writer Stephen Gaghan with his research.[2] Like *The Good Shepherd* (2006), released the following year, *Syriana* 'asks if something has gone wrong with the CIA post 9/11, or if anything about the Agency was ever right' (Jenkins 2012: 129). While making claims on truth, equally *Syriana* operates as a fictionalized political parable. Although clearly embedded in the politics of the Middle East, no specific territory is named, and instead the film points to the region in general. According to Gaghan, the word 'Syriana' is a 'term used by Washington think-tanks to describe a hypothetical reshaping of the Middle East'. For the film, Gaghan used the term in a more abstract way, dealing with how

'Syriana,' the concept – the fallacious dream that you can successfully remake nation-states in your own image – is a mirage. Syriana is a fitting title for a film that could exist at any time and be about any set of circumstances that deal with man's unchecked ambition, hubris, and the fantasy of empire.

(quoted in Warner Bros. Entertainment Inc. 2005: 11)

'Syriana' is, then, an idea rather than a place. Reviewers described the film as an 'evocation of a new world disorder' (Hoberman 2005b) and 'not so much a story as a malaise' (Denby 2005: 110).

Central to constructing this vision is the use of a network narrative structure weaving together four storylines linking the US government, intelligence service and energy business in a corrupt and violent battle to control dwindling oil resources. As part of the lead ensemble cast heading this multi-narrative structure, Clooney plays Bob Barnes, a veteran mid-level CIA field agent with years of experience conducting nefarious dealings in Middle East territories. When he starts criticizing the Agency's new policy directions for the region, Barnes becomes an embarrassment to his superiors. Before he is pulled out of the field completely, Barnes is sent to Beirut to organize the assassination of Prince Nasir Al-Subaai, son of Emir

Al-Subaai. Barnes is led to understand the kill is necessary because Nasir is funding terrorists, but the real reason for the Prince's removal is that if he succeeds his father as ruler, he'll introduce modernizing and democratizing reforms that include expelling US military and oil interests from his country. As a loyal servant, Barnes goes on the mission, but when the assassination goes wrong, he's disowned by the Agency. Realizing he's been set up, Barnes is trying to warn the Prince of the threat to his life when both are killed by a missile strike launched by the CIA. In a second story, Washington lawyer Bennett Holiday (Jeffrey Wright) must scrutinize a merger between Connex, a large energy company, and Killen, a small Texas company that has recently won a major contract to extract oil from Kazakhstan. After finding evidence that Killen channelled corrupt payments to a Kazak minister, Holiday must engineer a cover up to allow the merger to go through, and so he comes to realize his work was only required to give the illusion of due diligence. Third, energy analyst Bryan Woodman (Matt Damon) becomes chief economic advisor to Prince Nasir and is won over by the Prince's plans for reform. Those hopes are erased, however, when Nasir's younger brother is made Emir, and Woodman witnesses the Prince's death in the missile attack. Finally, Wasim Khan (Mazhar Munir), a Pakistani guest worker at the Connex plant in the emirate ruled by Al-Subaai, is made unemployed. After failing to find new employment, Khan and his friend Farooq (Sonnell Dadral) start attending a madrasa, where they are schooled in Islamic fundamentalist belief and come under the influence of Mohammed Sheik Agiza (Amr Waked) who recruits them to undertake a suicide attack against a tanker ship.

At no point do these four stories converge into a single narrative line; rather, loose linkages are made between them. This network organization is necessary to map the intricate and contradictory forces making up US–Middle East relations. Instead of mounting a central argument, the film is an elaboration on the tagline used to market the movie: 'Everything is connected.' As Barnes, Clooney has

the symbolic capital of artistic honours rather than the economic capital of revenue capture (McDonald 2013: 215–53). With *Syriana*, Clooney was nominated for an acting Oscar for the first time, and his portrayal of Barnes won the statue for Actor in a Supporting Role at the 78th Academy Awards ceremony.[4] After Clooney entered the elite of Oscar-winning actors, his status as a prestige star was affirmed with Actor in Leading Role nominations for *Michael Clayton, Up in the Air* (2009) and *The Descendants* (2011). In the case of *Syriana*, the award-winning status of Clooney's performance cannot be disassociated from its political significance. Historical trends suggest that in their voting, members of the Academy like to conflate seriousness of subject matter with seriousness of artistic standing. *Syriana* perfectly fit these twin demands, for Clooney's performance combined a timely critique of foreign policy with the spectacle of an actorly commitment to physical transformation. Chapter 2 already suggested that the heavy facial hair and weight gain used to represent Barnes created an 'anti-Clooney' Clooney performance. To a significant degree, the impact of Clooney's performance as Barnes does indeed come from how it broke with the familiar version of his star brand, and yet at the same time the performance consolidated the political meanings of the brand while confirming Clooney's graduation to prestige stardom. On-screen politics have therefore not only made Clooney a modern star of the Hollywood Left but have also supplied subject matter to give artistic gravitas to the brand.

Off-screen politics and Clooney's auto-critique of the star as magnifier

Picking up his Oscar for *Syriana*, Clooney used his speech to acknowledge how the Hollywood community might be disconnected from wider opinion but yet importantly functioned to draw attention to real world problems such as disease or discrimination.

You know, we are a little bit out of touch in Hollywood every once in a while, I think. It's probably a good thing. We're the ones who talk about AIDS when it was being whispered, and we talked about civil rights when it wasn't really popular. And we, you know, we bring up subjects, we are the ones – this Academy, this group of people gave Hattie McDaniel an Oscar in 1939 when blacks were still sitting in the backs of theatres. I'm proud to be a part of this Academy. I'm proud to be a part of it as a community. I'm proud to be out of touch.

(Oscars 2011)

Tensions and contradictions inevitably emerge when Hollywood movie stars flexibly spread their fame into off-screen contexts to offer political comment and critique. While Hollywood stardom can shed light on issues otherwise excluded from or ignored in the public sphere, at the same time questions of legitimacy always hang over whether someone so 'out of touch', whose claim to fame comes from representing other people in films, can hold the credentials necessary to qualify as an authoritative political spokesperson.

In November 2006, *People* magazine awarded Clooney the title of 'Sexiest Man Alive' for a second time. Celebrating this achievement, *People* ran it's 'sexy interview', asking Clooney questions about dating, his type of woman, whether he had any plans for marriage and kids, growing older, the art of wearing a tuxedo, his favourite cocktail, and the 'burden of being sexy'. Commenting on his appearance, the interviewer noted 'George Clooney is movie-star dazzling in an offhand way: jeans, scuffed Harley motorcycle boots, a black tee and a green rubber bracelet that reads "Not On Our Watch," a reference to his activism on behalf of the troubled Darfur region of Sudan' (Leonard 2006: 73). Throwing together star lifestyle with humanitarian crisis, this description encapsulates the contradictions of celebrity activism. Earlier the same year Clooney and his father had travelled to Darfur, the first of several journeys to Sudan to observe first-hand the humanitarian disaster arising from the ongoing civil war in the region. Rooted in government attempts to segregate Sudan's African and native Arab populations, the conflict involved the Sudanese military and indigenous Arab Janjaweed militias in attempts to supress guerrilla actions by rebel forces. Government violence spread beyond targeting the rebels, mounting a large-scale campaign of persecution against Darfur's non-Arab civilian population, with killings and the use of mass rape as a weapon of war. Escaping the conflict, millions were displaced to refugee camps, and hundreds of thousands died, many from the violence, although the majority from starvation and disease. In September 2004, the US Secretary of State Colin Powell declared the situation in Darfur an act of genocide (Kessler and Lynch 2004).

After reading about the crisis in a 2005 *The New York Times* column by Nicholas Kristof, and frustrated by the apparent lack of US action to halt the persecution in Darfur, Clooney called his father with a proposal: 'Listen I want to go over there … I'll go and be the famous guy and you be the reporter. I'll get us on the morning shows when we come back, and you cut the story' (quoted in Setoodeh 2014: 40). Following the journey in April 2006, Clooney shared a press conference at the National Press Club with Republican Senator Sam Brownback and Democrat Senator Barack Obama. Around 200 people, including three dozen photographers, gathered to hear Clooney say:

It is the first genocide of the 21st century. The president wants to put a stop to it. Congress wants to put a stop to it. The U.N. want to put a stop to it … What they need now is the American people and the world's population to help them, to tell them that it matters that much to us, that it's that important to us.

(quoted in Puzzanghera 2006)

Brownback had already spent two years campaigning for stronger US intervention in the conflict but admitted he'd never previously achieved anywhere near the same level of media attention. Clooney was clear about his role in the proceedings: 'I'm not a legislator. I'm not a politician ... I just try to use the credit card that you get for being famous in life in instances when I can' (quoted in Puzzanghera 2006). Obama, working with Brownback to sponsor legislation to increase funding for peacekeeping operations in Darfur, reflected: 'Whether we like it or not, we are a celebrity-obsessed culture. When we get a movie star involved, people pay more attention. It's better when the movie star actually knows what he's talking about ... [Clooney's] not just a pretty face' (quoted in Puzzanghera 2006).

Clooney's 2006 comments illustrate the contradictions of politicized celebrity. With what authority can someone known for being the 'Sexiest Man Alive' comment on something as catastrophic as genocide? Implicitly or explicitly, tensions between the superficial and deep, or the artificial and real, define the legitimization challenge confronting Hollywood stars when they engage with politics. As with his films, Clooney's off-screen politics is a mode of performance, and as with any performance, questions arise over how believable or credible the performance is. In celebrity politics, the performance always tests a star's capacity to convincingly present himself or herself as 'an "authentic," "ethical" self' (Totman and Marshall 2015: 604). Whenever Hollywood stars take to the political 'stage' their interventions inescapably unite politics, performance and publicity. As well-known figures, stars can make politics known, functioning to raise awareness, particularly when bringing attention and coverage to issues otherwise demoted or ignored in the news agendas of press and broadcast journalism. In this way, the star functions as 'magnifier': 'In a dispersed media ecology, the celebrity is a powerful force that perhaps better than any other practice/object identifies the operation of a contemporary attention economy: their physical proximity to an issue brings it alive as a political entity' (ibid. 603). What is maybe most interesting in Clooney's case is how he consistently articulates an open and heightened self-reflection on his status as mediator or magnifier of political meaning. Clooney knows he is a 'famous guy', useful for drawing media attention. On Darfur, he admits: 'My job is to amplify the voice of the guy who lives here and is worried about his wife and children being slaughtered' (quoted in Attewill 2011). Similarly, he's commented, 'I like the ability to shine light and make it loud' (quoted in Setoodeh 2014: 36). Clooney acknowledges that his fame forms a prism through which Western media have engaged with and represented the Darfur conflict: 'We put ourselves there because part of the story is that you're putting yourself in harm's way. That allows you to come back and do a junket with thirty news outlets – which makes a difference in the amount of attention you're generating for the cause' (quoted in Fussman 2012: 64). He openly declares his fame operates as a kind of 'capital' selectively invested to achieve certain returns: 'If celebrity is a credit card, then I'm using it … I knew I had to shine light on this situation' (quoted in Daunt 2007a: E5).

Stars can make politics known but then there is always the question of *how* they make politics known. While functioning as media magnifiers, concurrently there is the danger that a star may deflect attention from the substance of politics if the story becomes about the star and not the positions or policies. Again, Clooney is self-consciously aware of these potential pitfalls. Following their work on Darfur campaigning, Clooney and Obama built a personal friendship. When Obama first announced he'd run for presidential office, Clooney – mindful of how the prism of celebrity can not only deflect attention away from core policy issues but also negatively count against candidates – told the Senator 'I would do anything for him, including staying completely away from him' (quoted in Daunt 2007b: E19). When his father stood during 2004 as a Democrat candidate for the House of Representatives in the family's home state of Kentucky, Clooney held back from becoming involved in the campaign. Still, he blames his father's lack of success on how media reporting nevertheless engineered a divide that 'became an issue of Hollywood versus the heartland' (ibid. E1). It is therefore maybe unnecessary to theorize the political functions of Clooney's celebrity, for in many respects, he's already done it himself. Clooney has self-theorized the value and limits of a star's political capital. Upfront acknowledgment of the contradictions that surround awareness-raising is crucial to how Clooney has negotiated and managed the tensions of politicized celebrity. With the above quotes and other statements, Clooney has articulated an auto-critical, meta-commentary on the communicative function and symbolic power of politicized celebrity. In Clooney's case, the performance of ethical authenticity comes in part then from his frank and honest admissions about the role, limitations and potential downsides of the star as magnifier.

To a certain extent, Clooney's auto-critique anticipates and short circuits attacks on the legitimacy of politicized stardom, but only to a degree. Clooney is not alone in being subjected to condemnations of Hollywood liberalism from the conservative Right. For decades, opinion has commonly held there is institutionalized political bias in Hollywood and the US entertainment industry in general. Contemporary Hollywood has had its share of big-name conservatives – Charlton Heston, Clint Eastwood, Heather Locklear, Chuck Norris, Arnold Schwarzenegger, Bruce Willis, Mel Gibson – but the majority of stars to openly declare political allegiances have aligned themselves with the Left, most notably by promoting humanitarian causes or articulating anti-war sentiments. Consequently, conservative opinion has organized against liberal Hollywood and its star representatives. In a dig at liberal supremacy in the entertainment industries, Republican Senator John McCain once remarked: 'If Washington is a Hollywood for ugly people, Hollywood is a Washington for the simple-minded' (quoted in Goldstein 2003: E4). Conservatives allege the entertainment business is not only politically skewed but also indulges in conspiratorial 'blacklisting'. 'Even Albania has two political parties but not Hollywood,' complains David Horowitz, director of the

Center for the Study of Popular Culture and vocal conservative activist: 'Liberalism is like a religion in Hollywood. If you aren't a liberal, you're a heretic' (quoted in Heyman 2000: 25).[5] 'Those who make their home in Tinseltown,' alleges James Hirsen, columnist for the 'Left Coast Report' carried on right-wing website Newsmax. com, 'quickly find out that when it comes to the A-list, you're either left or you're left out' (2004: 3). *New York Post* columnist Andrea Peyser refers to Hollywood liberals as 'celebutards', a pejorative portmanteau neologism connecting celebrity, debutant and retard. For Peyser, celebutards are 'lazy and egotistical thinkers, stars equipped with abundant money, fame, idle hours and yes-men, who feel secure enough in their own influence and intelligence to create insane foreign or domestic policy' (2009: 2). Conservatives claim bullying by liberal professional colleagues has produced a political subculture in Hollywood (Bond 2008; Engel 2008; Johnson 2016). Aimed at highlighting contradictions between the elite privileged lifestyles of stars and the disempowered they speak of and for, 'limousine liberals' is an epithet frequently deployed to discredit and delegitimize the Hollywood Left. 'For conservatives on the lucrative warpath,' notes James Wolcott (2006: 108) in *Vanity Fair*, 'celebrity liberals are the favorite lunchmeat. Big-game hunters need big-names to hunt, familiar heads to add to their trophy collection.'

As a self-proclaimed liberal, Clooney is a choice target for these attacks. In Peyser's opinion 'Clooney has translated his public adulation into an annoying willingness to express whatever offensive or inane liberal patter crosses his graying head' (2009: 30), and *Good Night, and Good Luck* was a 'socially conscious, historically illiterate propaganda picture' (ibid. 28). In an original take on how Clooney's flexible stardom traverses the film market (see Chapter 3), Peyser asserts Clooney 'intends to continue making political balderdash – interspersed with money-making movies' (ibid. 35). Hirsen has joined in the slamming of Clooney's political films: by showing soldiers attempting to steal gold, *Three Kings* was in his eyes part of a wave of late-1990s films, including *Courage Under Fire* (1996) and *The Thin Red Line* (1998), 'obsessed with portraying the military in a negative light' (2004: 233). Similarly, Hirsen (2006: 246) regarded *Syriana* as 'terrorist-sympathizing', and rather than attempting to draw complex connections between Big Oil, the CIA and Middle Eastern sovereignty, was 'simply a two-hour long disjointed left-wing fantasy' (ibid. 247). Despite *Good Night, and Good Luck* using archival footage of Joe McCarthy actually speaking, Hirsen says the senator appeared in as 'a shallow, cartoonish, and demonic figure'. He accuses the film of ignoring evidence from Soviet communications decrypted as part of the Venona Project 'revealing that McCarthy's basic premise that Communists had infiltrated our government was not only right, it was underestimated' (ibid. 248).[6]

Conservative attacks on liberal Hollywood consistently highlight and exploit the contradictions of politicized stardom. As Wolcott (2006: 110) notes, conservative opinion has characterized Clooney as 'a slick phony, a sanctimonious ham, and the perfect cuspidor for their contempt ... embod[ying] the smarmy liberal ethos of elitist Hollywood'. Confronting these attacks, Clooney's auto-critique operates as a kind of defence mechanism against partisan opinion. Again, he is his own self-theorizer. Rather than shirking from those attacks, Clooney has adopted a stance of anticipating and confronting the inevitable disparagement and condemnation: 'We can't demand freedom of speech then turn around and say, But please don't say bad things about us. You gotta be a grown up and take your hits. I am a liberal. Fire away' (reproduced at PalJoey 2006).

Stars and labour

Clooney's communicative function as magnifier sees him articulating personal views or arguments to defend the interests of others. When occupying this position, Clooney's off-screen engagements with a

appeal, leaving Judge Walker's ruling in place, and clearing the way for the recommencement of same-sex marriage in California.

Reiterating the responsibilities of politicized stardom, Clooney has said 'I [think] that my job is to try and find ways of talking about issues that move us forward ... That's what you can do as a celebrity. You don't make policy. But you can shine a light on faulty or good policy' (quoted in Daunt 2007a: E5). Without any formal political office, Clooney plays no direct part in policy-making, although calls have come from several quarters for Clooney to stand for elected office. Speaking of his client, publicist Stan Rosenfeld once remarked 'He looks presidential' (ibid.). Regardless, Clooney has declined to stand, and has decisively distanced himself from the formal operations of policy formation. Happy to 'shine a light' on issues, he dismisses the idea of entering political office: 'boy, the idea of administering and legislating. What a nightmare' (quoted in Setoodeh 2014: 36). 'I have absolutely no political ambitions,' he's declared. Demonstrating awareness of how the realm of professional politics puts anyone under a spotlight where moral rectitude is interrogated as a measure of professional integrity, Clooney has joked that if he were to stand 'I'd have to run on a completely different ticket than anyone else ever ran on. I'd have to run on the "Yeah, I did it" ticket. "Did you sleep with so-and-so?" "Yeah, I did." "Did you take drugs?" "You bet I did" ' (quoted in Hoberman 2005a). Paradoxically here, the work of auto-critique performs a responsible and ethical self precisely by disclosing an irresponsible and unethical self. 'I didn't live my life in the right way for politics,' he admits, 'I fucked too many chicks and did too many drugs and that's the truth' (quoted in Attewill 2011). Integrity is created not by presenting a pure character but conversely by revealing a morally compromised self through confessional performance.

Rather than enter political office, Clooney has engaged with party politics from a distance, donating to, and fundraising for, the campaigns of Democrat candidates during periods of electioneering.

In 2008 and 2012, Clooney attended fundraising galas in Geneva for the election and re-election of Obama as president (Daunt 2008c; Nebehay 2012). Further support for Obama's 2012 re-election came when Clooney opened his Los Angeles home to hosting a fundraising dinner. Full-price admission cost $40,000, with an online competition run for members of the general public to win tickets. Although some of the proceeds were donated to the re-election campaign, the majority share went to the Democratic National Committee (DNC) (Johnson 2012; Keegan 2012). Hollywood political fundraising events produce a concentrated focus for the contradictions of celebrity politics. Congregating ostentatious wealth and privilege, Hollywood fundraisers can become morally sensitive events, occasions where clear divisions are demarcated between the 'haves' and the 'have nots'. Such events therefore have to balance financial gain against the danger of losing grassroots voters. These sensitivities erupted in April 2016 when Clooney ran another high-priced dinner at his home in support of the Hillary Victory Fund, a joint fundraising committee for the DNC and Hillary Clinton's campaign to become the Democrat presidential candidate. Tickets cost $33,400 for an individual and up to $353,400 for a couple. Right-wing media seized the moment to highlight the celebrity extravagance. At the same time Senator Bernie Sanders, Clinton's Democrat rival, emailed his supporters, calling the money paid 'obscene' and appearing on CNN to say:

I have a lot of respect for George Clooney. He's a great actor. I like him. But this is the problem with American politics … Big money is dominating our political system. And [my supporters and I] are trying to move as far away from that as we can … So it's not a criticism of Clooney. It's a criticism of a corrupt campaign finance system, where big money interests – and it's not Clooney, it's the people coming to this event – have undue influence on the political process.

(CNN 2016)

Clooney responded on NBC's *Meet the Press*, agreeing the amount of money in politics was indeed obscene. Rather than paying for the Clinton campaign, he explained the majority share of proceeds went to support the Democrats in efforts to reclaim Congress, thereby putting the party in a position where it could potentially overturn precisely the legislation permitting such large amounts of money to go into politics. Pointing to the levels of funding available to Republicans, specifically to donations promised by super-wealthy industrialists Charles and David Koch, Clooney argued the current system regrettably made it necessary for Democrats to play the same game, (NBC News 2016).

With this line of justification, Clooney's auto-critique moved beyond himself and towards the general place of celebrity within an overall system of party funding. Adopting a defensive position, however, Clooney arguably struggled to find a persuasive rationalisation. For example, user comments accompanying the posting of the Clooney–NBC interview on YouTube are indicative of wider sentiments that question the political legitimacy of stars. '2020Max1' commented, 'The only difference between Clooney and the Koch brothers is that one gives obscenely to Democrats and the other gives obscenely to Republicans'. Questioning the legitimacy of Clooney to speak on these matters, 'Dick Johnson' asked, 'Who cares what he thinks', to which 'Jack Swift' offered a pithy reply summarizing the contradictions of politicized stardom: 'Exactly. The fucker was in "Batman and Robin" afterall … ' (see NBC News 2016).

Humanitarian star

Finally, the Darfur crisis is just one case where Clooney has used the 'credit card' of celebrity to 'shine a light' on humanitarian causes. Repeatedly he has either coordinated and/or participated in telethons for raising monies to help those suffering from the consequences of human or natural disaster (Brill 2003). Starting with *America: A Tribute to Heroes* (2001) for families affected by the 9/11 terror attacks, he subsequently worked on *Tsunami Aid* (2005) for victims of the 2004 Indian Ocean earthquake, *Shelter from the Storm* (2005) to fund relief efforts after Hurricane Katrina, and *Hope For Haiti Now* following the 2010 earthquake. Exercising the power of cross-promotion, in May 2007 the premiere of *Ocean's Thirteen* was used to publicize the launch of Not On Our Watch (NOOW), a charitable foundation established by Clooney and other members of the film's cast – Don Cheadle, Matt Damon and Brad Pitt – and its producer Jerry Weintraub (Glaister 2007). NOOW has remained 'committed to robust advocacy and research in support of global human rights. Drawing upon figures with powerful voices, [to] develop projects and campaigns that bring global attention to forgotten international crises' (Not On Our Watch n.d.). To surveil the situation in Darfur, from 2010 to 2015 the Satellite Sentinel Project (SSP) operated as a partnership between anti-genocide activist organization the Enough Project and commercial satellite operator DigitalGlobe. Co-founded by Clooney and Enough's John Prendergast, the purpose of the SSP was to conduct 'monitoring of both Sudan and South Sudan to assess the human security situation, identify potential threats to civilians, and detect, deter and document war crimes and crimes against humanity' (SSP 2014). Funded primarily by NOOW, the SSP operated under the banner 'The world is watching because you are watching'. Clooney described the project as 'the antigenocide paparazzi': 'We want them to enjoy the level of celebrity attention that I usually get' (quoted in Benjamin 2010). 'How is it,' he complained, 'you can Google Earth my house and anybody can take a picture of me anytime, anywhere, and you can't do that with a war criminal' (quoted in Cohen 2014: 61). Combining on-the-ground field research conducted by Enough, with satellite imagery and geospatial analysis provided by DigitalGlobe, the SSP produced evidence of mass graves, troop and weapon movements, forced displacement, and village razings, using this as the basis for reports released to the press and through a network of activists on social media. On another note, in April 2016 Clooney travelled to commemorate the Armenian Meds Yeghern, the killing of 1.5 million Armenians by the Ottoman Empire over a century before. Despite the scale of the atrocity, most nations worldwide, including the US, have yet to formally recognize this act of ethnic cleansing as genocide. Speaking in the Armenian capital Yerevan, Clooney said 'we honour those lives by calling their tragedy by its true name. Genocide. The Armenian Genocide' (quoted in Amos 2016). The occasion was also used to host the first presentation of the Aurora Prize for Awakening Humanity, in which NOOW partnered and Clooney co-chaired the selection committee. Aside from the causes in which Clooney has personally been involved, he's also made donations to multiple other charities and foundations (Table 4.1).

Clooney has become a humanitarian star, not only in the sense of being a movie star who lends his fame to humanitarian causes, but also by how accumulated prestige has seen him become an esteemed luminary honoured in the institutional contexts of organized humanitarianism. Just as Clooney has acquired a Golden Globe, Oscar and other awards for his work as an actor, his activist work, principally concerning Darfur, has seen him accrue the symbolic capital of humanitarian prestige. In 2007, the World Summit of Nobel Peace Prize Laureates awarded Clooney and Don Cheadle with the Peace Summit Award, conferred annually on 'personalities from the world of culture and entertainment who actively stand up for peace and make broader audiences aware of issues in the contemporary world' (World Summit of Nobel Peace Laureates n.d.a). Clooney and Cheadle were honoured for 'their strong engagement in favour of pacification in the tortured Darfur region, for having contributed to saving human lives and to alleviating the suffering of the civil populations victims of the war' (World Summit of Nobel Peace Laureates n.d.b). Folding Clooney into the institutional structure of

Table 4.1 Charities and Foundations Supported by Clooney

Charities and Foundations	Purpose
21st Century Leaders	'support[s] humanitarian and environmental causes, striving to encourage a generation of influencers to take ownership, positive action and raise awareness among their fans for global causes'
American Foundation for AIDS Research	'accelerating the pace of HIV/AIDS research and achieving real breakthroughs'
American Foundation for Equal Rights	'fought for full federal marriage equality for all Americans'
Andrea Bocelli Foundation	'mission is to empower people and communities in situations of poverty, illiteracy, distress due to illness and social exclusion'
Ante Up For Africa	'poker tournament organized by Don Cheadle and Annie Duke aimed at raising money and public awareness for the crisis in Darfur'
Barbara Davis Center for Childhood Diabetes	'provid[ing] state-of-the-art care to children and adults with type 1 diabetes'
CARE	'works around the globe to save lives, defeat poverty and achieve social justice'
Casey Lee Ball Foundation	'mission is to educate the public concerning pediatric kidney disorders and to promote organ donor awareness and kidney research'
Cinema for Peace	'promot[ing] worldwide peace and understanding through the support of cinematographic works'
Clothes Off Our Back	'charity auctions showcasing today's hottest celebrity attire … with proceeds going to benefit children's charities'
Enough Project	'seeks to build leverage for peace and justice in Africa by helping to create real consequences for the perpetrators and facilitators of genocide and other mass atrocities'
Entertainment Industry Foundation	'rais[ing] awareness and funds for critical health, educational and social issues in order to make a positive impact in our community and throughout the nation'
Everyone Matters	'encourag[ing] people to judge others less, while at the same time accepting ourselves for who we are, without shame or judgment'
Feeding America	'feed[ing] America's hungry through a nationwide network of member food banks'
International Rescue Committee	'responds to the world's worst humanitarian crises and helps people whose lives and livelihoods are shattered by conflict and disaster'
Make-A-Wish Foundation	'to grant the wishes of children with life-threatening medical conditions to enrich the human experience with hope, strength and joy'
Make It Right	'builds homes, buildings and communities for people in need'

Charities and Foundations	Purpose
Make Poverty History	'building healthy homes for communities in need'
Motion Picture and Television Fund Foundation	'supports [the] entertainment community in living and aging well, with dignity and purpose, and in helping each other in times of need'
Not On Our Watch	'committed to robust advocacy and research in support of global human rights'
ONE Campaign	'taking action to end extreme poverty and preventable disease, particularly in Africa'
Onyx and Breezy Foundation	'saving lives of animals every day'
Oxfam	'working to find lasting solutions to poverty, suffering and injustice'
Partners in Health	'work[ing] in close partnership with local government officials and the world's leading medical and academic institutions to build capacity and strengthen health systems'
Realizing the Dream	'seek[ing] to continue the legacy and work of [Martin Luther and Coretta Scott] King in wiping out poverty and injustice through programs that foster peace and nonviolent social change, empower poverty-stricken communities, and develop strong leaders among the nation's youth'
Red Cross	'prevents and alleviates human suffering in the face of emergencies by mobilizing the power of volunteers and the generosity of donors'
Rock For Darfur	'series of concerts organised by MySpace.com and Oxfam to benefit Oxfam's relief efforts in Sudan and neighbouring Chad'
Satellite Sentinel Project	'conducts monitoring of both Sudan and South Sudan to assess the human security situation, identify potential threats to civilians, and detect, deter and document war crimes and crimes against humanity'
Save the Children	'in the United States and around the world, [giving] children a healthy start, the opportunity to learn and protection from harm'
Screen Actors Guild Foundation	'providing... comprehensive, educational and state-of-the-art resources to SAG-AFTRA members'
Small Steps Project	'supporting children around the world who live on rubbish dumps and survive from scavenging'
Stand Up To Cancer	'aims to raise money for cancer researchers and scientists to come together and reach their common goal'
United Nations Children's Fund (UNICEF)	'works in 190 countries and territories to save and improve children's lives, providing health care and immunizations, clean water and sanitation, nutrition, education, emergency relief'
United Way	'improves lives by mobilizing the caring power of communities around the world to advance the common good'
Whatever It Takes	'artwork project which inspires hope by gathering artworks from leaders in all fields; royalty, film, music, Nobel Peace Prize laureates, sports, literature'
World Food Programme	'world's largest humanitarian agency fighting hunger'

Sources: compiled from Look to the Stars (2017) and websites of the respective charities and foundations.

international diplomacy, in 2008 the actor was designated as one of the UN's Messengers of Peace, 'distinguished individuals, carefully selected from the fields of art, literature, science, entertainment, sports or other fields of public life, who have agreed to help focus worldwide attention on the work of the United Nations' (United Nations n.d.). Clooney was twice nominated but never won an Emmy for his work on *ER*; however, in 2010 the Academy of Television Arts and Sciences' Board of Governors conferred on him the Bob Hope Humanitarian Award, reserved for 'an individual in the telecommunications industry whose humanitarian work has brought credit to the industry and whose deeds and actions have a lasting impact on society' (ATAS 2010). Clooney received the award for his efforts in mobilizing the entertainment industry through the aforementioned telethons. In October 2013, the Shoah Foundation's Institute for Visual History and Education at the University of Southern California, dedicated to archiving testimonies of historical genocides, awarded Clooney its Ambassador for Humanity Award (Grossberg 2013). Finally, in a meeting of religious and entertainment celebrity, in May 2016 Pope Francis presented Clooney at the Vatican with a 'Medal of the Olive' (San Martín 2016).

Humanitarian stardom can bring media exposure to marginalized issues yet may equally undermine understanding of the complexities involved if the media coverage becomes about the star's individualized experience of crisis rather than the underlying causes and circumstances. This contradiction is illustrated by the documentary *A Journey to Darfur*, constructed using footage from when Clooney and his father visited the country, and aired in January 2007 on the AmericanLife TV Network (Figure 4.2). A short running length prevented the documentary from conducting any detailed explanation or analysis of the political circumstances behind the conflict, and along the way certain pieces of significant information are left out, such as China's supply of weapons to the Sudanese government in return for oil. On the one hand, the film tells the story of Darfur, relating the background to the conflict,

Figure 4.2 Humanitarian stardom. Clooney magnifies media coverage of crisis in *A Journey to Darfur* ('A Journey to Darfur' directed by Larry Herskowitz © The Nostalgia Network, Inc. 2007. All rights reserved).

offering testimonies from villagers affected by the crisis, showing the work of humanitarian aid agencies, and campaigning by the Save Darfur Coalition. On the other, the film is the story of the Clooneys, outlining the motivations behind their trip, how they stealthily entered Sudan, their interactions with villagers, and their efforts to raise awareness once they returned to the US. Both stories are told, but as the 'journey' title would suggest, the Clooney trip provides the main throughline for narrativizing the events and the prism through which those events are made comprehensible. *A Journey to Darfur* therefore condenses the contradictions of politicized stardom. Without the involvement of George Clooney, it's highly unlikely the film would have been made or aired. Even if only one person who saw the film learnt of things they didn't know before, then it helped raise consciousness of suffering by the Darfuris. At the same time, the experiences of beleaguered Africans arc mediated through the white Western point of view. Like *Three Kings* (see pp. 130–1), arguably the film turns humanitarian care into a white saviour narrative.

By cultivating belief in exceptional individualism, film stardom generally masks the collective efforts required for producing stardom (McDonald 2013: 12–14). Similarly, the focus on the singular personality obscures the collective work that goes into the making of the humanitarian star. As with his acting stardom, Clooney's humanitarian stardom is a creation of cooperative working. Given limited capacity for film stars to speak with knowledge and authority in the political realm, high-profile names in Hollywood have co-opted expertise by hiring the services of political consultants.

Hired by moguls and movie stars, they act as the conduits between show business and Washington power. Largely former campaign staffers and political aides – of the Democratic variety, of course – they coach their clients on who matters in D.C. ... What these consultants sell ... is leverage and access.

(Snyder 2007: 118)

Brokering connections to Washington is important but political consultants also provide the specialized knowledge necessary to brief and advise their clients on the issues dearest to their hearts. For this purpose, Clooney has accessed the expertise of civil rights lawyer David Pressman (Daunt 2008a and 2008b). After working on post-genocide transitional justice issues for the Supreme Court of Rwanda, Pressman became an aide to US Secretary of State Madeleine Albright and then worked for the American Civil Liberties Union. Pressman was the architect of Clooney's Darfur mission. It was after leading an advocacy initiative to raise international awareness of, and campaign for, action on Darfur that Pressman facilitated the first trip by the Clooneys to the region. Organizing publicity opportunities once the Clooneys returned, Pressman acknowledged the role of star as magnifier.

The media has been a dismal failure in telling the story of the first genocide of the twenty-first century. While Darfur can't generate news, George Clooney can. Wherever he goes, cameras follow. I wanted to get Darfur into the news, to build political capital for our political leaders to take action. However uncomfortable one may be about celebrity interaction with political/humanitarian causes, the people I met in Darfur needed a voice and George Clooney has a powerful one.

(quoted in NYU | Law n.d.)

The second significant figure in the making of Clooney's humanitarian stardom is the human rights activist John Prendergast. In his own right Prendergast became a star of humanitarian action, acquiring expertise in African affairs over a career which, since the mid-1980s, saw him work for the Clinton administration, the US State Department, two members of Congress, the National Intelligence Council, UNICEF, Human Rights Watch, the International Crisis Group, and the US Institute of Peace (APB Speakers International 2015). Through his work, Prendergast developed several connections with Hollywood humanitarians. In 2003, he organized for Angelina Jolie to travel to Eastern Congo, ravaged by five years of civil war, and subsequently co-authored two books on Darfur with Don Cheadle. He became a board member and Strategic Advisor for NOOW, and as the founder of the Enough Project, collaborated with Clooney in establishing the SSP and co-authoring op-ed pieces for *The Washington Post, Time, Vice News*, and *The New York Times* (Clooney and Prendergast 2010; Clooney and Prendergast 2011; Clooney and Prendergast 2014; Clooney, Prendergast and Kumar 2015). As much as the engagement with politics can test the legitimacy of film stars, so Prendergast believes associations with Hollywood can tarnish credibility in the political sphere.

It does take a toll in the snobbish Washington circles ... Some people think you're not serious because you hang out with celebrities. They don't

understand that the only way you can make a difference is by reaching as many people as possible ... People like Angelina [Jolie] and George Clooney are catalysts. Every time they spend an hour on a cause, it could inspire a 1,000 new activists. They bring fresh and intelligent discourse to the debate.
(quoted in Daunt 2007c: E24)

Clooney's role as magnifier or catalyst inevitably encourages a focus on the individual as the agent of conscience and action. Even once the scope is expanded to include Pressman and Prendergast, a vision is still created in which humanitarian action is understood to be the work of a few dedicated figures. As Asteris Huliaras and Nikolaos Tzifakis (2012: 418) argue, this results in the perception 'that celebrities operate somehow autonomously in transnational politics and attempt to generate change through the elaboration and operationalization of individual strategies'. Huliaras and Tzifakis show how Clooney's original engagement with Darfur came nearly two years after the Save Darfur Coalition had been working to focus world attention on the genocide. Supported by over 180 humanitarian, human rights and religious organizations, the Coalition represented what Huliaras and Tzifakis call a 'transnational advocacy network' (419). In their analysis Huliaras and Tzifakis trace how statements by Clooney closely echoed frames of meaning already applied by the Coalition, and so argue Clooney was a 'latecomer' to a cause already actioned through a network of international support. Reflecting on this particular instance, they arrive at a more general conclusion, that arguments for or against the value 'of celebrity activism overestimate the individual influence of these players' (427).

Even though Clooney came late to the cause, the communicative prism of Hollywood stardom attracted coverage of the Darfur crisis through channels otherwise inaccessible to the Coalition. But this leaves open the most challenging question of humanitarian stardom: just how far does the raising of awareness translate into action and change? For his part in the Darfur activist movement, Clooney's

CONCLUSION: 'THE LAST MOVIE STAR'

Speaking to a BBC reporter in March 2016, about three months before his fifty-fifth birthday, Clooney explained that as age caught up with him, he'd got to a point in his career where he was considering no longer acting in films: 'As you age on-screen you get to that point where you really understand that, you know, you can't stay in front of the camera, you know, your whole life' (BBC 2016). Instead, he was planning to do more directing. Age is a key determinant of Hollywood stardom. Even in the post-studio system, Hollywood stars must be regarded as products, figures created for circulation in media markets. One of the anthropomorphic metaphors popularized in marketing theory is the 'product life cycle', by which goods are seen to pass through phases of launch, growth, maturity and decline. There are reasons to question whether brands follow the same trajectory or otherwise transcend the tests of time (Kapferer 2012: 214–15). Still, movie star brands would seem to follow a similar arc: actors who later become stars launch careers and establish a set of meanings for which they are known, then grow their fame as awareness of them increases, and once they've 'made it' their status stabilizes and matures. Stardom has a finite 'shelf life', however, for not only are actors mortal, but as their value is contingent on the film market, star status wanes as market trends move in other directions leaving them behind. Star maturity therefore inevitably presages decline. In the BBC interview, Clooney reflected:

I think nobody really wants to see anybody really age. You know it's a very unforgiving thing the camera is and so ageing becomes something that you, you know, try to do less and less on-screen, you know, you try to pick the films that work best for you and as you age they become less and less.

(BBC 2016)

Hollywood stardom is age sensitive. It is widely acknowledged that in Hollywood film, working opportunities for female actors, including the very few who receive industry recognition as stars, become ever more limited once they pass the age of thirty. History shows that Hollywood is more generous to male stars, some of whom carry on working and maintaining their elevated status into their fifties, but eventually they must accept their leading status has gone (McDonald 2013: 30).

Clooney's honest assessment of his own status reflects on the more general age patterning of Hollywood stardom. Beyond a story of individual decline, however, we might read Clooney's waning status as a synecdoche for wider change in Hollywood. Clooney's BBC interview contemplated his own individual situation, but that situation would now seem to reflect on Hollywood stardom more broadly. Not only individual stars, but Hollywood stardom as a cultural institution, appears to have aged and entered a period of decline. Stars perform in the film market as signs of economic value. Only very briefly, and intermittently, with the hits *The Perfect Storm* (2000) and the *Ocean's* trilogy (2001, 2004 and 2007), released when he was at the end of his thirties and into his mid-forties, did Clooney seem to operate as a lucrative attraction. As these films featured Clooney as a member of core ensembles of mainly male actors, however, it would seem wise to exercise caution and avoid attributing too much of that commercial success to his presence. *Gravity* (2013) was a major hit but Clooney had only a supporting role to Sandra Bullock. Clooney ranked in the Quigley poll of top money-making stars for a final time when he came second in 2011, although his two releases that year – *The Ides of March* (grossing $76 million worldwide) and *The Descendants* (selling $177.2 million worth of tickets) – were hardly hits. After peaking in the popular film market, the 'mature' Clooney brand settled into the speciality market.

Clooney's diminished box office value comes in a period when star-driven films no longer lead the box office. In the last decades of the twentieth century, star-centred films were regularly appearing among the highest grossing hits for any year. Since the start of the new millennium, however, fantasy-based franchise films and feature-length animated hits have defined popularity at the worldwide box office. Certain actors have gained considerable exposure and financial returns through franchise movies, although their inability to score similar levels of commercial success when working outside the franchise strongly suggests audiences are prepared to pay for the franchise concept more than the actors who appear in it. Consequently, among Hollywood insiders, there is now a lack of belief in the commercial value of stars (McDonald 2013: 134–7). Instead of marking the hits, star-driven movies – if this is still a fair label – belong to secondary or tertiary tiers of box office popularity. Featuring Clooney alongside Julia Roberts, *Money Monster* (2016) had the appearance of a showcase for a former era of Hollywood stardom. Respectively aged fifty-five and forty-eight when the film was released, Clooney and Roberts might have been regarded as 'past it'. As part of the core ensemble casts, both had scored hits the previous decade with *Ocean's Eleven* (2001) and *Ocean's Twelve* (2004). When Roberts was paid $20 million for *Erin Brockovich* (2000), she set a new high point for pay among female stars, although subsequently her price dropped: after all she was all of 32 years old when *Erin Brockovich* was released! *Money Monster* was a critical disappointment, although the $93.3 million it grossed worldwide was a respectable if not amazing performance for a drama about the precarious and nefarious dealings of the financial sector, made on a relatively low budget reported to be in the region of $27 million.

It has been the purpose of the preceding chapters to see Clooney as the exemplar of post-studio stardom in modern Hollywood and that role must now be extended to include recognition of Clooney as a symbol of the decline of Hollywood stardom. For her biography of Clooney, entertainment writer Kimberly Potts (2007) chose the title *George Clooney: The Last Great Movie Star*. Writing for *Look* magazine, reporter Chris Nashawaty (2005) used the title 'The Last Great Movie Star' for a profile of Clooney. With his article on hosting Clooney for dinner in his own home, journalist Joel Stein (2008) landed the cover of *Time* with a picture of Clooney and the main line 'The Last Movie Star'. These writings never explained why Clooney should be considered the last star: maybe it was presumed to be self-evident that Clooney is, or was, a star of the period in Hollywood history when stardom in general declined.

Long before that BBC interview when Clooney disclosed he was contemplating pulling back from acting, the power of Hollywood stardom was already in decline. It is impossible to tell if this is a passing phase, a transitory market trend, and whether at a future date stars will once again have an important role to play in selling popular film. In the meantime, it could be asked: is Clooney starring in the finale to Hollywood stardom? On that cover of *Time*, Clooney presented one of his best homages to old Hollywood stardom, seated beside his swimming pool and characteristically dressed in a light-grey suit jacket and white open-collar shirt with his hair slicked and parted. With its multiple allusions to the past, the Clooney brand is shrouded in nostalgia, yet possibly the most significant contribution that this brand may make to Hollywood stardom is the nostalgia it evokes for stardom itself.

APPENDIX: BUDGET AND RATINGS FOR CLOONEY'S FILMS (1996–2016) [1]

	Production Budget [2] ($m)	MPAA Average Negative Cost [3] ($m)	CARA Rating [4]
From Dusk Till Dawn	19	36.4	R
One Fine Day	n/a	36.4	PG
Batman & Robin	125	39.8	PG-13
The Peacemaker	50	39.8	R
Out of Sight	48	53.4	R
Three Kings	75	52.7	R
The Perfect Storm	140	51.5	PG-13
O Brother, Where Art Thou?	26	51.5	PG-13
Ocean's Eleven	85	54.8	PG-13
Solaris	47	47.7	PG-13
Intolerable Cruelty	60	47.8	PG-13
Ocean's Twelve	110	66.3	PG-13
Syriana	50	65.7	R
The Good German	32	63.6	R
Ocean's Thirteen	85	65.8	PG-13
Michael Clayton	21	65.8	R
Leatherheads	58	70.8	PG-13
Burn After Reading	37	70.8	R

	Production Budget [2] ($m)	MPAA Average Negative Cost [3] ($m)	CARA Rating [4]
The Men Who Stare at Goats	25	n/a	R
Up in the Air	25	n/a	R
The American	20	n/a	R
The Descendants	20	n/a	R
The Monuments Men	70	n/a	PG-13
Money Monster	27	n/a	R

Notes

[1] Includes all theatrically released feature films between 1996 and 2016 in which Clooney took lead or lead ensemble roles, and so does not include *The Thin Red Line, Spy Kids, Welcome to Collinwood, Confessions of a Dangerous Mind, Spy Kids 3-D, Good Night, and Good Luck, The Ides of March, Gravity, Tomorrowland* and *Hail, Caesar!*, and voice work for *South Park: Bigger, Longer & Uncut* and *Fantastic Mr. Fox*.

[2] Reported production budget. Source: boxofficemojo.com

[3] Annual average budget for films produced by MPAA members. Sources: MPA 2006: 18; MPAA 1998, 1999, 2000 and 2008: 7.

[4] CARA rating for release in the US. Source: filmratings.com

BIBLIOGRAPHY

Academy Originals (2015) 'The Story of the Ocean's Eleven Costumes',
   29 June. Available at: https://www.youtube.com/watch?v=VypMOlWTP8o
   (accessed 28 February 2017).

Access Hollywood (2012) 'George Clooney: "At Some Point, Gay
   Marriage Won't Be An Issue"', 12 November. Available at: https://www.
   accesshollywood.com/articles/george-clooney-at-some-point-gay-
   marriage-wont-be-an-issue-66192/ (accessed 28 February 2017).

ACTING!!! (2014) 'George Clooney Bobbles His Head', 10 September.
   Available at: www.youtube.com/watch?v=RZgUclE5J-w (accessed
   28 February 2017).

Adams, J. (2015) *The Cinema of the Coen Brothers: Hard-Boiled Entertainments*.
   New York: Columbia University Press.

Alleva, R. (2016) 'Spectacle and Speculation', *Commonweal*, 17 June,
   pp. 19–20.

Amos, H. (2016) 'George Clooney Visits Armenia to Meet President, Talk
   Genocide', *International Business Times*, 25 April. Available at: http://
   www.ibtimes.com/george-clooney-visits-armenia-meet-president-talk-
   genocide-2358953 (accessed 28 February 2017).

Ansen, D. (1998) 'The Fugitive Falls in Love', *Newsweek*, 29 June, p. 66.

APB Speakers International (2015) 'John Prendergast: International
   Affairs Expert'. Available at: http://www.apbspeakers.com/speaker/john-
   prendergast (accessed 28 February 2017).

ArgueLab.com (2015) 'The Secret to the Voices of George Clooney and Morgan Freeman', 10 August. Available at: https://www.youtube.com/watch?v=vnSjF6iRyLk (accessed 28 February 2017).

ATAS (2010) 'George Clooney to Receive Bob Hope Humanitarian Award', 21 July. Available at: http://www.emmys.com/news/latest-news/george-clooney-receive-bob-hope-humanitarian-award (accessed 28 February 2017).

Attewill, F. (2011) 'Clooney: Sex Life Bars Me from Politics', *Metro*, 24 February, p. 6.

Baer, R. (2002) *See No Evil: The True Story of a Ground Solider in the CIA's War on Terrorism*. London: Arrow.

Baker, A. (2015) 'Why George Clooney is Supporting Coffee Farming in South Sudan', *Time*, 12 June. Available at: http://time.com/3918857/george-clooney-south-sudan/ (accessed 28 February 2017).

Baker, J. (2013) 'Elmore Leonard: "I Don't Write Comedy … But the Humor is There"', *The Oregonian*, 24 August. Available at: www.oregonlive.com/books/index.ssf/2013/08/jeff_baker_elmore_leonard_i_do.html (accessed 28 February 2017).

Baumann, S. (2007) *Hollywood Highbrow: From Entertainment to Art*. Princeton, NJ: Princeton University Press.

BBC (2003) 'Clooney in Anti-war Protest', *BBC News*, 20 January. Available at: http://news.bbc.co.uk/1/hi/entertainment/2677881.stm (accessed 28 February 2017).

BBC (2016) 'George Clooney Says It Is Time to Quit Acting', 1 March. Available at: http://www.bbc.co.uk/news/entertainment-arts-35669917 (accessed 28 February 2017).

Benjamin, M. (2010) 'Clooney's "Antigenocide Paparazzi": Watching Sudan', *Time*, 28 December. Available at: http://content.time.com/time/printout/0,8816,2040211,00.html (accessed 28 February 2017).

Bernstein, A. (1997) 'Batman & Robin', *Drama-Logue*, 26 June, p. 28.

BFI (n.d.) 'Definition of Specialised Film'. Available at: http://www.bfi.org.uk/sites/bfi.org.uk/files/downloads/bfi-definition-of-specialised-film-bfi-neighbourhood-cinema-2016-01.pdf (accessed 28 February 2017).

Bond, P. (2008) 'Hollywood's Dartboard?', *The Hollywood Reporter*, 20 October, pp. 1 and 12.

Borrelli, C. (2010) 'Why George Clooney Always "Plays Himself" in Movies', *Chicago Tribune*, 5 March. Available at: http://articles.chicagotribune. com/2010-03-05/entertainment/sc-mov-0302-art-of-playing-yourself-20100305_1_movie-star-range (accessed 28 February 2017).

Brennan, J. (1996) 'Mr Freeze is Heating Up Hollywood's Money Race', *Los Angeles Times*, 15 July, pp. F1 and 8.

Brill, S. (2003) 'How Hollywood Responded to 9/11', *Daily Variety*, 11 June, p. 52.

Brodesser, C. (2000) 'Willis Makes Waves to "Oceans 11"', *Daily Variety*, 25 May, p. 7.

Brodie, J. (1995) 'Playing Doctor', *GQ*, March, pp. 196–201.

Busch, A. M. (1995) 'Crusader Clooney', *Daily Variety*, 24 October, pp. 1 and 16.

Busch, A. M. (1997a) 'Lopez: $2 mil in Sight for "Out of Sight"', *Daily Variety*, 15 May, p. 3.

Busch, A. M. (1997b) 'Soderbergh to Helm Clooney', *Daily Variety*, 3 March, pp. 1 and 60.

Busch, A. M. (1997c) 'WB, Clooney Take "Kisses"', *Daily Variety*, 28 July, pp. 1 and 21.

Busch, A. M. and Dawtry, A. (1996) 'Clooney Fitted for Batsuit', *Daily Variety*, 23 February, pp. 1 and 76.

Byrge, D. (1996) 'One Fine Day', *The Hollywood Reporter*, 2 December, pp. 9 and 14.

Byrge, D. (1997a) 'Batman & Robin', *The Hollywood Reporter*, 16 June, pp. 8 and 40.

Byrge, D. (1997b) 'The Peacemaker', *The Hollywood Reporter*, 22 September, pp. 5 and 14.

CARA (n.d.a) 'The Film Ratings System'. Available at: http://filmratings.com/ downloads/mpaa_ratings-poster-qr.pdf (accessed 28 February 2017).

CARA (n.d.b) 'What: Guide to Ratings'. Available at: http://filmratings.com/ what.html (accessed 28 February 2017).

Carman, E. (2016) *Independent Stardom: Freelance Women in the Hollywood Studio System*. Austin, TX: University of Texas Press.

Carson, T. (2007) 'The Heppest Cat Around', *GQ*, June, pp. 114–20.

CERVECERIA SCHOPPEN (2013) 'Budweiser® George Clooney Narrates for the Famous Budweiser 2005 flv video free file download at fliiby com',

13 February. Available at: www.youtube.com/watch?v=7D_oz25ko9Q (accessed 28 February 2017).

Rockonjuju, Chaîne de (2006) 'Nespresso Commercial – George Clooney –What Else', 5 July. Available at: https://www.youtube.com/watch?v=DfyeXrdZZ1o (accessed 28 February 2017).

Charity, T. (1996) 'From Dusk Till Dawn', *Time Out*, 29 May, p. 65.

Clooney, G. and Prendergast, J. (2010) 'George Clooney and John Prendergast: We Can Prevent the Next Darfur', *The Washington Post*, 17 October. Available at: http://www.washingtonpost.com/wp-dyn/content/article/2010/10/15/AR2010101503871_pf.html (accessed 28 February 2017).

Clooney, G. and Prendergast, J. (2011) 'Famine as a Weapon: It's Time to Stop Starvation in Sudan', *Time*, 8 December. Available at: http://time.com/3059803/george-clooney-sudan-starvation/ (accessed 28 February 2017).

Clooney, G. and Prendergast, J (2014) 'Sudan's Silent Suffering is Getting Worse', *Vice News*, 11 June. Available at: https://news.vice.com/article/sudans-silent-suffering-is-getting-worse (accessed 28 February 2017).

Clooney, G., Prendergast, J. and Kumar, A. (2015) 'George Clooney on Sudan's Rape of Darfur', *The New York Times*, 25 February. Available at: http://www.nytimes.com/2015/02/26/opinion/george-clooney-on-sudans-rape-of-darfur.html?_r=0 (accessed 28 February 2017).

Clooneyfiles (2007) 'George Clooney – No Martini No Party', 7 January. Available at: https://www.youtube.com/watch?v=PDhyst6Kq4U (accessed 28 February 2017).

CNN (2016) 'Sanders: Clooney Fundraiser is "Obscene"', 27 March. Available at: https://www.youtube.com/watch?v=JyjQJk0M4yQ&feature=youtu.be (accessed 28 February 2017).

Cohen, D. S. (2000) 'Creating an Atypical "Storm" Watch', *Daily Variety (Showbiz Expo)*, 23 June, pp. A24 and 26.

Cohen, D. S. (2014) 'Clooney Turns Spotlight on Bad Actors', *Variety*, 12 August, pp. 61–2.

Conant, J. (1996) 'Heartthrob Hotel', *Vanity Fair*, December, pp. 274–8 and 326–8.

Corliss, R. (1996) 'Quentin: Is He Orson Yet?', *Time*, 29 January, p. 72.

Cox, D. (1995) '"Dawn" for Clooney, Tarantino', *Daily Variety*, 17 April, pp. 3 and 18.

Cox, D. and Fleming, M. (1999) 'Warners Will Play Ball With Clooney "Spy"', *Daily Variety*, 31 March, pp. 1 and 15.

Cunneff, T. and Feldon-Mitchell, L. (1995) 'Long Day's Gurney', *People*, 16 January, pp. 92–5.

D'Alessandro, A. (2006) 'Domestic Top 250 of 2005', *Variety*, 9 January, 52–3.

Daniels, B., Leedy, D. and Sills, S. D. (2006) *Movie Money: Understanding Hollywood's (Creative) Accounting Practices* 2nd edn. Los Angeles: Silman-James.

Dargis, M. (1996) 'Blood Brothers', *LA Weekly*, 19 January, p. 35.

Daunt, T. (2007a) 'Fame? Priceless', *Los Angeles Times*, 19 June, pp. E1 and 5.

Daunt, T. (2007b) 'For Now He'll Just Wait in the Wings', *Los Angeles Times*, 30 March, pp. E1 and 19.

Daunt, T. (2007c) 'Helping Hollywood Get Serious About Africa', *Los Angeles Times*, 12 January, pp. E1 and 24.

Daunt, T. (2008a) 'Celebs' Wonks May Go to D.C.', *Los Angeles Times*, 28 November, pp. E1 and 10.

Daunt, T. (2008b) 'George Clooney Depends on "Cuz"', *Los Angeles Times*, 2 May, pp. E1 and 18.

Daunt, T. (2008c) 'Obama's Swiss Bash', *Los Angeles Times*, 8 August, pp. E1 and 15.

David Horowitz Freedom Center (2016) 'About David Horowitz Freedom Center'. Available at: http://www.horowitzfreedomcenter.org/about (accessed 28 February 2017).

Davies, J. (2005) '"Diversity. America. Leadership. Good Over Evil." Hollywood Multiculturalism and American Imperialism in *Independence Day* and *Three Kings*', *Patterns of Prejudice*, 39 (4), pp. 397–415.

Denby, D. (2005) 'Company Man', *The New Yorker*, 5 December, pp. 109–11.

DePaulo, L. (2000) 'Catch Him If You Can', *Vogue*, June, pp. 184–93.

Dunkley, C. (1997) 'Clooney Sets "Sight" for Uni After "Batman"', *The Hollywood Reporter*, 11 February, pp. 1 and 75.

Dyer, R. (1998) *Stars*. London: British Film Institute.

clooney-receives-usc-shoah-foundations-ambassador-for-humanity-award/
(accessed 28 February 2017).

Gutfeld, G. (2006) 'George Clooney: I am a Celebrity! There, I Said It!',
The Huffington Post, 13 March. Available at: http://www.huffingtonpost.
com/greg-gutfeld/george-clooney-i-am-a-cel_b_17231.html (accessed
28 February 2017).

Harris, P. (2005) 'How a Heart-throb Became the Voice of Liberal America',
The Observer, 27 November, p. 14.

Heyman, J. D. (2000) 'Hollywood Republicans Remain the Minority', *US*,
28 August, pp. 24–7.

Heynothinyoucansay (2008) 'NO MARTINI - NO PARTY - GEORGE
CLOONEY - SPOT- ANUNCIO', 9 March. Available at: https://www.
youtube.com/watch?v=utElXdS4Piw (accessed 28 February 2017).

Hindes, A. (1998) 'D'Works Lock Up "Castle"', *Daily Variety*, 17 September,
p. 1.

Hirsen, J. (2004) *Tales from the Left Coast: True Stories of Hollywood Stars and
their Outrageous Politics*. New York: Three Rivers.

Hirsen, J. (2006) *Hollywood Nation: Left Coast Lies, Old Media Spin, and the
New Media Revolution*. New York: Three Rivers.

Hoberman, J. (1996) 'Border Crossings', *Village Voice*, 30 January, p. 41.

Hoberman, J. (2005a) 'Celebrity Journalist', *Village Voice*, 5 October, p. 32.

Hoberman, J. (2005b) 'Spy Game', *Village Voice*, 23 November, p. 61.

Hollywood Reporter, The (1999) 'Storm Dies for Cage', 29 March, p. 8.

Holson, L. M. (2005) 'Confessions of a Perplexed Mind', *The New York Times
(Business)*, 17 January, pp. 1 and 4.

Hontz, J. (1998) 'Clooney Cloned', *Daily Variety*, 19 June, pp. 1 and 68.

Hontz, J. (1999) 'Clooney Sitcom Goes to HBO', *Daily Variety*, 3 February,
pp. 1 and 27.

Huliaras, A. and Tzifakis, N. (2012) 'The Fallacy of the Autonomous Celebrity
Activist in International Politics: George Clooney and Mia Farrow in
Darfur', *Cambridge Review of International Affairs*, 25 (3), pp. 417–31.

Hunter, D. (1996) 'From Dusk Till Dawn', *The Hollywood Reporter*,
18 January, pp. 12 and 72.

Jenkins, T. (2012) *The CIA in Hollywood: How the Agency Shapes Film and Television*. Austin, TX: University of Texas Press.

Johnson, J. and Orange, M. (2004) *The Man Who Tried to Buy the World: Jean-Marie Messier and Vivendi Universal*. London: Penguin.

Johnson, T. (1996a) 'Clooney in Deal at WB', *Daily Variety*, 22 November, pp. 1 and 64.

Johnson, T. (1996b) 'Clooney's Nom de Shingle: Left Bank', *Daily Variety*, 6 December, p. 5.

Johnson, T. (2012) 'Clooney to Host Obama', *Daily Variety*, 11 April, p. 3.

Johnson, T. (2016) 'Red in a Sea of Blue', *Variety*, 26 April, pp. 50–1.

Johnston, S. (2000) 'O Brother, Where Art Thou?', *Screen International*, 19 May, p. 24.

Joyner, J. (2006) 'I am a Liberal. There, I Said It!', *Outside the Beltway*, 13 March. Available at: http://www.outsidethebeltway.com/george_clooney_i_am_a_liberal/ (accessed 28 February 2017).

Junger, S. (2000) 'Watching Hollywood Brew a "Perfect Storm"', *The New York Times*, 30 April. Available at: http://www.nytimes.com/2000/04/30/movies/summer-films-action-watching-hollywood-brew-a-perfect-storm.html (accessed 28 February 2017).

Junod, T. (2013) 'George Clooney's Rules for Living', *Esquire*, December, pp. 124–30 and 177.

Kapferer, J. (2012) *The New Strategic Brand Management: Advanced Insights and Strategic Thinking* 5th edn. London: Kogan Page.

Karon, P. (1997a) 'Clooney Tunes Prod'n Pipeline', *Daily Variety*, 19 August, pp. 1 and 18.

Karon, P. (1997b) 'WB Takes "Long Walk" for Clooney's Maysville', *Daily Variety*, 21 October, pp. 5 and 22.

Karon, P. and Petrikin, C. (1998) 'Petersen Set to Track "Storm" Pic', *Daily Variety*, 28 January, pp. 1 and 26.

Kaufman, A. (2005) 'George Clooney', *Daily Variety (Eye on the Oscar: The Director)*, 6 December, p. A5.

Kauffmann, S. (1997) 'Seeing Is, Initially, Believing', *The New Republic*, 3 November, p. 28.

Keegan, R. (2012) 'Stars Align as the Wind Shifts', *Los Angeles Times*, 10 May, pp. D1 and 9.

Kemper, T. (2010) *Hidden Talent: The Emergence of Hollywood Agents*. Berkeley, CA: University of California Press.

Kessler, G. and Lynch, C. (2004) 'U.S. Calls Killings in Sudan Genocide', *The Washington Post*, 10 September. Available at: http://www.washingtonpost.com/wp-dyn/articles/A8364-2004Sep9.html (accessed 28 February 2017).

King, G. (2005) *American Independent Cinema*. London: I B Tauris.

King, G. (2016) *Quality Hollywood: Markers of Distinction in Contemporary Studio Film*. London: I B Tauris.

Kit, B. (2006) 'Clooney Has Smoke with Heslov, WB', *The Hollywood Reporter*, 20 July, pp. 1 and 19.

Kit, Z. (1999a) 'Clooney Finds "Storm" for WB, Petersen', *The Hollywood Reporter*, 18 May, pp. 3 and 92.

Kit, Z. (1999b) '"Sight" Lines: Clooney, Soderbergh Eyeing Prod'n Deal at Warner Bros.', *The Hollywood Reporter*, 2 December, p. 2.

Kit, Z. (2001) 'Uni Exec Fox to Section Eight', *The Hollywood Reporter*, 15 June, pp. 6 and 41.

Koehler, R. (2006) 'Surgeon of Own Career', *Daily Variety (VPlus)*, 13 October, pp. A2 and 6.

Lambert, S. (1997) 'Batman & Robin', *Boxoffice*, August, p. 50.

Landesman, C. (2000) 'Rules of Engagement', *The Sunday Times*, 5 March, pp. 8–9.

Lane, A. (1997a) 'Summer Olympics: "Men in Black," "Batman & Robin," "Hercules," etc.' *The New Yorker*, 7 July, pp. 76–8.

Lane, A. (1997b) 'Going Nuclear', *The New Yorker*, 6 October, p. 125.

Lane, A. (1998) 'Jack Be Quick', *The New Yorker*, 6 July, pp. 78–9.

Landler, M. (2014) 'U.S. is Facing Hard Choices in South Sudan', *The New York Times*, 3 January. Available at: http://www.nytimes.com/2014/01/04/us/politics/us-is-facing-hard-choices-in-south-sudan.html (accessed 28 February 2017).

Langer, J. (1981) 'Television's Personality System', *Media, Culture and Society*, 3 (4), pp. 351–65.

Leonard, E. (2006) 'The Sexy Interview: George Clooney', *People*, 27 November, pp. 72–80.

Levy, E. (1998) 'Out of Sight', *Daily Variety*, 22 June, pp. 4 and 22.

Look to the Stars (2017) 'George Clooney: Charity Work, Events and Causes'. Available at: https://www.looktothestars.org/celebrity/george-clooney (accessed 21 January 2017).

Lowry, B. (1994) 'What's New on the Networks', *Daily Variety*, 30 August, pp. 26, 28, 31–2.

McClintock, P. (2005) 'What's Eight Minus Two?' *Variety*, 28 November, p. 8.

McCarthy, T. (1996a) '"Dusk": A Bigscreen Dawn for Clooney', *Variety*, 22 January, pp. 98 and 100.

McCarthy, T. (1996b) 'Pfeiffer, Clooney Strike "Fine" Balance', *Variety*, 2 December, p. 65.

McCarthy, T. (1997a) 'Freeze Frames Push Icy "Batman"', *Variety*, 16 June, pp. 34 and 37.

McCarthy, T. (1997b) 'The Peacemaker', *Daily Variety*, 22 September, pp. 2 and 18.

McCarthy, T. (2000) 'Prisoners Lock up the Charm in Coens' Southern Escapade', *Variety*, 22 May, pp. 19 and 32.

McDonald, P. (2000) *The Star System: Hollywood's Production of Popular Identities*. London: Wallflower.

McDonald, P. (2004) 'Why Study Film Acting: Some Opening Reflections', in C. Baron, D. Carson and F. P. Tomasulo (eds) *More Than a Method: Trends and Traditions in Contemporary Film Performance*. Detroit: Wayne State University Press, pp. 23–41.

McDonald, P. (2012a) 'Spectacular Acting: On the Exhibitionist Dynamics of Film Star Performance', in J. Sternagel, D. Levitt and D. Mersch (eds) *Acting and Performance in Moving Image Culture: Bodies, Screens, Renderings*. Bielefeld: Transcript, pp. 61–70.

McDonald, P. (2012b) 'Story and Show: The Basic Contradiction of Film Star Acting', in A. Taylor (ed.) *Theorizing Film Acting*. London: Routledge, pp. 169–83.

McDonald, P. (2013) *Hollywood Stardom*. Malden, MA: Wiley-Blackwell.

McDonald, P. (2017) 'Flexible Stardom: Contemporary American Film and the Independent Mobility of Star Brands', in G. King (ed.) *A Companion to American Indie Film*. Malden, MA: Wiley Blackwell, pp. 493–520.

McLean, T. J. (2006) 'Section Eight Goes Up in Smoke', *Daily Variety (VPlus)*, 13 October, pp. A2 and 6.

McNary, D. (2001) 'Jumping Off Ban Wagon', *Daily Variety*, 25 October, pp. 1 and 21.

McNary, D. (2008) 'Peacemaker?', *Daily Variety*, 27 June, pp. 1 and 21.

McNulty, C. (2012) 'Stars Power "8"', *Los Angeles Times*, 5 March, pp. D1 and 8.

Marhsall, P. D. (1997) *Celebrity and Power: Fame in Contemporary Culture*. Minneapolis: University of Minnesota Press.

Maslin, J. (1996) 'Enough Blood to Feed the Thirstiest Vampires', *The New York Times*, 19 January. Available at: http://www.nytimes.com/1996/01/19/movies/film-review-enough-blood-to-feed-the-thirstiest-vampires.html (accessed 28 February 2017).

Maslin, J. (1997) 'The Cold War is Back, Nuclear Bombs and All', *The New York Times*, 26 September, p. E10.

MER (2003) 'MER Comment', *Mid-East Realities*, 12 February. Available at: http://www.middleeast.org/launch/redirect.cgi?num=243&a=15 (accessed 28 February 2017).

Moerk, C. (2000) 'Clooney's First of "11"', *Daily Variety*, 10 January, pp. 1 and 47.

Morgenstern, J. (1996) 'Film: Vampires and Victorians', *The Wall Street Journal*, 26 January, p. A9.

Morgenstern, J. (1997) 'Film: Looking for Mr. Goodcat', *The Wall Street Journal*, 20 June, p. A16.

MPA (2006) *US Entertainment Industry: 2005 MPA Market Statistics*. Washington: MPA Worldwide Market Research and Analysis.

MPAA (1998) *1997 US Economic Review: Theatrical Data*. Washington, DC: Motion Picture Association of America. Available at: >http://www.mpaa.org./useconomicreview/1997/theatrical2.htm> (accessed 11 February 1999).

MPAA (1999) *1998 Economic Review*. Washington, DC: Motion Picture Association of America.

MPAA (2000) *1999 US Economic Review*. Washington, DC: Motion Picture Association of America.

MPAA (2008) *Entertainment Industry Market Statistics 2007*. Washington: Motion Picture Association of America.

Nashawaty, C. (2005) 'The Last Great Movie Star', *Look*, December, pp. 44–9.

NBC News (2016) 'George Clooney on Why He's Not Like the Koch Brothers', *Meet the Press*, 18 April. Available at: https://www.youtube.com/watch?v=c-1XoojLorE (accessed 28 February 2017).

Neale, S. (2000) *Genre and Hollywood*. London: Routledge.

Nebehay, S. (2012) 'Clooney Star Guest at Obama Fundraiser in Switzerland', *Reuters*, 27 August. Available at: http://www.reuters.com/article/entertainment-us-usa-campaign-obama-cloo-idUSBRE87Q0RO20120828 (accessed 28 February 2017).

Not on Our Watch (n.d.) 'Who We Are'. Available at: http://notonourwatchproject.org/who_we_are (accessed 28 February 2017).

NYU | Law (n.d.) 'Alumnus/Alumna of the Month: David Pressman '04'. Available at: http://www.law.nyu.edu/alumni/almo/pastalmos/20062007almos/davidpressmannovember#interview (accessed 28th February 2017).

Oscars (2011) 'George Clooney Wins Supporting Actor: 2006 Oscars', 31 March. Available at: www.youtube.com/watch?v=NqDbG9h-f7c (accessed 28 February 2017).

PalJoey (2006) 'GEORGE CLOONEY: "I Am a Liberal. There, I Said It!"', *broadwayworld.com*, 13 March. Available at: http://www.broadwayworld.com/board/readmessage.php?thread=889966&boardid=2 (accessed 28 February 2017).

Pearlman, C. (1997) 'Gorgeous George', *McCall's*, November, pp. 59–62.

Perry, A. (2014) 'George Clooney, South Sudan and How the World's Newest Nation Imploded', *Newsweek*, 10 October. Available at: http://europe.newsweek.com/george-clooney-south-sudan-how-worlds-newest-nation-imploded-274547?rm=eu (accessed 28 February 2017).

Peyser, A. (2009) *Celebutards: The Hollywood Hacks, Limousine Liberals, and Pandering Politicians Who Are Destroying America*. New York: Citadel.

Petrikin, C. (1999) 'Clooney, Lawrence Split Maysville,' *Daily Variety*, 30 September, p. 5.

Simmons, L. (2008) 'Clooney Enters the Fray', *The Hollywood Reporter*, 27 June, pp. 1 and 36.

Smith, D. (2015) 'South Sudan to Export Coffee for the First Time', *The Guardian*, 8 October. Available at: https://www.theguardian.com/world/2015/oct/08/south-sudan-export-coffee-beans-first-time-clooney (accessed 31 August 2016).

Snyder, G. (2007) 'Party Lines', *W*, May, pp. 118–20.

Sony Pictures (2009) 'Sony Pictures Entertainment to Ink Deal with George Clooney and Grant Heslov's Smokehouse Pictures', 30 June. Available at: http://www.sonypictures.com/corp/press_releases/2009/06_09/06302009_SPE_Smokehouse.html (accessed 30 June 2016).

Sragow, M. (1996) 'Isn't It Pedantic?' *New Times Los Angeles*, 19 December, p. 30.

SSP (2014) 'Human Security Alert: Massive Mobilization of SAF in the Nuba Mountains', *Satellite Sentinel Project*, 15 April. Available at: http://www.satsentinel.org/press-release/human-security-alert-massive-mobilization-saf-nuba-mountains (accessed 28 February 2017).

Stein, J. (2004) 'The Wiz of Showbiz', *Time*, 6 December, pp. 100–06.

Stein, J. (2008) 'Guess Who Came to Dinner?', *Time*, 3 March, pp. 46–52.

Street, J. (2004) 'Celebrity Politicians: Popular Culture and Political Representation', *British Journal of Politics and International Relations*, 6 (4), pp. 435–52.

Totman, S. and Marshall, P. D. (2015) 'Reel/Real Politics and Popular Culture', *Celebrity Studies*, 6 (4), pp. 603–06.

Travers, P. (2005) 'See It Now', *Rolling Stone*, 20 October, p. 89.

Turan, K. (1996) '"Fine Day" a Dawning for Clooney,' *Los Angeles Times*, 20 December, pp. F1 and 20.

Turan, K. (1997a) 'Dreamboat Diplomacy', *Los Angeles Times*, 26 September, pp. F1 and 16.

Turan, K. (1997b) 'Meanwhile, Back at the Batcave … ' *Los Angeles Times*, 20 June, pp. F1 and 12.

Tyrangiel, J. (2005) '"So, You Ever Killed Anybody?"', *Time*, 21 November, pp. 132–5.

Tyson, J. (n.d.) 'How Movie Distribution Works,' *HowStuffWorks*. Available at: http://entertainment.howstuffworks.com/movie-distribution1.htm (accessed 28 February 2017).

Tyson, P. (n.d.) 'Read Venona Intercepts', *Secrets, Lies, and Atomic Spies*. Available at: http://www.pbs.org/wgbh/nova/venona/intercepts.html (accessed 28 February 2017).

Tzioumakis, Y. (2013) *Hollywood's Indies: Classics Divisions, Specialty Labels and the American Film Market*. Edinburgh: Edinburgh University Press.

United Nations (n.d.) 'About Messengers of Peace', *United Nations Messengers of Peace*. Available at: http://outreach.un.org/mop/the-messengers-of-peace-programme/ (accessed 28 February 2017).

Variety (2008) 'Domestic Top 250 of 2007,' 7 January, pp. 14–15.

Vera, H. and Gordon, A. M. (2003) *Screen Saviors: Hollywood Fictions of Whiteness*. Lanham, MD: Rowman and Littlefield.

Vincent, M. (1998) 'Is Superstar Status In Sight For Clooney?', *Orlando Sentinel*, 27 June. Available at: http://articles.orlandosentinel.com/1998-06-27/lifestyle/9806260621_1_rosemary-clooney-nick-clooney-miguel-ferrer (accessed 28 February 2017).

Vivendi Universal SA (2003) 'Form 424(b)(3) – Prospectus', 1 December. Available at: http://www.sec.gov/Archives/edgar/data/1127055/000115697303001819/u46864b3e424b3.htm (accessed 28 February 2017).

Vogel, H. L. (2007) *Entertainment Industry Economics* 7th edn. Cambridge: Cambridge University Press.

Warner Bros (2003) 'Section Eight Television Signs Two Year Pact With Warner Bros. Television' 30 July. Available at: http://www.warnerbros.com/studio/news/section-eight-television-signs-two-year-pact-warner-bros-television (accessed 30 June 2016).

Warner Bros. Entertainment Inc. (2005) Press book for *Syriana*.

Wasser, F. (2001) *Veni, Vidi, Video: The Hollywood Empire and the VCR*. Austin, TX: University of Texas Press.

WatchMojo.com (2015) 'Top 10 Actors With Voices Women Find Sexy', 7 March. Available at: www.youtube.com/watch?v=iBOXoiyXlE8 (accessed 28 February 2017).

Waxman, S. (2005) *Rebels on the Backlot: Six Maverick Directors and How They Conquered the Hollywood Studio System*. New York: HarperCollins.

West, K. (2007) 'George and Renée', *W*, December, pp. 302–06.

Whitaker, B. (2000) 'Actors Strike Against Radio and Television Advertisers', *The New York Times*, 2 May. Available at: http://www.nytimes. com/2000/05/02/business/actors-strike-against-radio-and-television-advertisers.html?_r=0 (accessed 28 February 2017).

Wilonsky, R. (2000) 'Bona Fide', *New Times Los Angeles*, 21 December, pp. 32–3.

Wolcott, J. (2006) 'It's Not Easy Being George', *Vanity Fair*, July, pp. 108–12, 140–1.

World Summit of Nobel Peace Laureates (n.d.a) 'Peace Summit Award'. Available at: http://www.nobelforpeace-summits.org/peace-summit-award/ (accessed 28 February 2017).

World Summit of Nobel Peace Laureates (n.d.b) 'Peace Summit Award 2007: Don Cheadle & George Clooney'. Available at: http://www.nobelforpeace-summits.org/portfolio/2007-doncheadle-georgeclooney/ (accessed 28th February 2017).

FILMOGRAPHY

Feature Films

Chronologically ordered according to the North American theatrical release date. Distributor details are for the North American release.

AND THEY'RE OFF (Theodore H. Kuhns III, USA, 1982)

Production: Summit Films. Distribution: unreleased. Role: uncredited

GRIZZLY II: THE CONCERT (aka PREDATOR: THE CONCERT) (André Szöts, USA, 1987)

Production: Harlequin Pictures. Distribution: unreleased. Role: uncredited

RETURN TO HORROR HIGH (Bill Froehlich, USA, 1987)

Production: Balcor Film Investors, New World Pictures. Distribution: New World Pictures. Role: Oliver

RETURN OF THE KILLER TOMATOES! (John De Bello, USA, 1988)

Production: Transatlantic Entertainment, Four Square Productions, Tomatoes II Productions. Distribution: New World Pictures. Role: Matt Stevens

RED SURF (H. Gordon Boos, USA, 1990)

Production: Arrowhead Entertainment. Distribution: Arrowhead. Role: Remar

THE HARVEST (David Marconi, USA, 1992)

Production: Curb Musifilm, Ron Stone Productions, THMPC. Distribution: Curb/Esquire Films. Role: Lip Syncing Transvestite

THE MAGIC BUBBLE (aka UN-BECOMING AGE) (Alfredo and Deborah Ringel, USA, 1992)

Production: Ringelvision Entertainment. Distribution: Castle Hill
   Productions. Role: Mac
FROM DUSK TILL DAWN (Robert Rodriguez, USA, 1996)
Production: Dimension Films, A Band Apart, Los Hooligans Productions,
   Miramax Films. Distribution: Dimension. Role: Seth Gecko
ONE FINE DAY (Michael Hoffman, USA, 1996)
Production: 20th Century Fox, Fox 2000 Pictures, Via Rosa Productions.
   Distribution: 20th Century Fox. Role: Jack Taylor
BATMAN & ROBIN (Joel Schumacher, USA/UK, 1997)
Production: Warner Bros., PolyGram Filmed Entertainment. Distribution:
   Warner Bros. Role: Batman/Bruce Wayne
THE PEACEMAKER (Mimi Leder, USA/UK, 1997)
Production: DreamWorks Pictures. Distribution: DreamWorks. Role:
   Lieutenant Colonel Thomas Devoe
OUT OF SIGHT (Steven Soderbergh, USA, 1998)
Production: Universal Pictures, Jersey Films. Distribution: Universal. Role:
   Jack Foley
THE THIN RED LINE (Terrence Malick, USA, 1998)
Production: Fox 2000 Pictures, Geisler-Roberdeau, Phoenix Pictures.
   Distribution: 20th Century Fox. Role: Captain Charles Bosche
SOUTH PARK: BIGGER LONGER & UNCUT (Trey Parker, USA,
   1999)
Production: Comedy Central Films, Scott Rudin Productions, Braniff
   Productions. Distribution: Paramount Pictures. Voice: Dr Gouache
THREE KINGS (David O. Russell, USA, 1999)
Production: Warner Bros. Pictures, Village Roadshow Pictures, Village-A.M.
   Partnership, Coast Ridge Films, Atlas Entertainment. Distribution:
   Warner Bros. Role: Archie Gates
THE PERFECT STORM (Wolfgang Petersen, USA, 2000)
Production: Warner Bros. Pictures, Baltimore Spring Creek Pictures, Radiant
   Productions. Distribution: Warner Bros. Role: Billy Tyne
O BROTHER, WHERE ART THOU? (Joel Coen, USA/UK/France, 2000)

Production: Universal Pictures, Touchstone Pictures, StudioCanal, Working
   Title, Mike Zoss Productions. Distribution: Buena Vista. Role: Ulysses
   Everett McGill
SPY KIDS (Robert Rodriguez, USA, 2001)
Production: Dimension Films, Troublemaker Studios. Distribution:
   Dimension. Role: Devlin
OCEAN'S ELEVEN (Steven Soderbergh, USA, 2001)
Production: Warner Bros. Pictures, Village Roadshow Pictures, NPV
   Entertainment, Jerry Weintraub Productions, Section Eight, WV Films II
   LLC. Distribution: Warner Bros. Role: Danny Ocean
WELCOME TO COLLINWOOD (Anthony and Joe Russo, USA/Germany,
   2002)
Production: Pandora, Warner Bros. Pictures, H5B5 Media AG, Section
   Eight, Gaylord Films LLC. Distribution: Warner Bros. Role: Jerzy
SOLARIS (Steven Soderbergh, USA, 2002)
Production: 20th Century Fox, Lightstorm Entertainment. Distribution:
   20th Century Fox. Role: Chris Kelvin
CONFESSIONS OF A DANGEROUS MIND (George Clooney, USA/
   Germany/Canada, 2002)
Production: Miramax Films, Mad Chance, Section Eight, Renaissance Films,
   JVS GmbH & Co. OHG. Distribution: Miramax. Role: Jim Byrd
SPY KIDS 3-D: GAME OVER (Robert Rodriguez, USA, 2003)
Production: Dimension Films, Troublemaker Studios. Distribution:
   Dimension. Role: Devlin
INTOLERABLE CRUELTY (Joel Coen, USA, 2003)
Production: Universal Pictures, Imagine Entertainment, Alphaville, Mike
   Zoss Productions. Distribution: Universal. Role: Miles Massey
OCEAN'S TWELVE (Steven Soderbergh, USA, 2004)
Production: Warner Bros. Pictures, Village Roadshow Pictures, Jerry
   Weintraub Productions, Section Eight, WV Films III LLC. Distribution:
   Warner Bros. Role: Danny Ocean
GOOD NIGHT, AND GOOD LUCK (George Clooney, USA/France/UK/
   Japan, 2005)

Production: Warner Independent Pictures, 2929 Entertainment, Participant
Productions, Davis Films, Redbus Pictures, Tohokushinsha, Section
Eight, Good Night Good Luck LLC. Distribution: Warner Independent
Pictures. Role: Fred Friendly

SYRIANA (Stephen Gaghan, USA/UAE, 2005)

Production: Warner Bros. Pictures, Participant Productions, 4M, Section
Eight. Distribution: Warner Bros. Role: Bob Barnes

THE GOOD GERMAN (Steven Soderbergh, USA, 2006)

Production: Warner Bros. Pictures, Section Eight, Virtual Studios.
Distribution: Warner Bros. Role: Jake Geismer

OCEAN'S THIRTEEN (Steven Soderbergh, USA, 2007)

Production: Warner Bros. Pictures, Village Roadshow Pictures, Jerry
Weintraub Productions, Section Eight, WV Films III LLC. Distribution:
Warner Bros. Role: Danny Ocean

MICHAEL CLAYTON (Tony Gilroy, USA, 2007)

Production: Samuels Media, Castle Rock Entertainment, Mirage
Enterprises, Section Eight, Clayton Productions LLC. Distribution:
Warner Bros. Role: Michael Clayton

LEATHERHEADS (George Clooney, USA/Germany, 2008)

Production: Universal Pictures, Casey Silver Productions, Smokehouse,
Internationale Scarena Filmproduktionsgesellschaft 1. Distribution:
Universal. Role: Dodge Connelly

BURN AFTER READING (Joel and Ethan Coen, USA/UK/France, 2008)

Production: Focus Features, StudioCanal, Relativity Media, Working Title,
Mike Zoss Productions. Distribution: Focus Features. Role: Harry Pfarrer

THE MEN WHO STARE AT GOATS (Grant Heslov, USA/UK, 2009)

Production: Overture Films, Winchester Capital Management, BBC Films,
Smokehouse, Ruby Films, Domino Pictures, Ingenious Film Partners,
UK Film Council, Westgate Film Services LLC. Distribution: Overture
Films. Role: Lyn Cassady

FANTASTIC MR. FOX (Wes Anderson, USA, 2009)

Production: 20th Century Fox, Indian Paintbrush, Regency Enterprises,
American Empirical Pictures. Distribution: 20th Century Fox. Voice: Mr Fox

UP IN THE AIR (Jason Reitman, USA, 2009)

Production: Paramount Pictures, Cold Spring Pictures, DW Studios, The Montecito Picture Company, Rickshaw Productions, Right of Way Films. Distribution: Paramount. Role: Ryan Bingham.

THE AMERICAN (Anton Corbijn, USA/UK, 2010)

Production: Focus Features, This Is That Productions, Greenlit Rights, Smokehouse. Distribution: Focus Features. Role: Jack/Edward

THE IDES OF MARCH (George Clooney, USA, 2011)

Production: Exclusive Media Group, Cross Creek Pictures, Crystal City Entertainment, Smokehouse, Appian Way. Distribution: Columbia. Role: Governor Mike Morris

THE DESCENDANTS (Alexander Payne, USA, 2011)

Production: Fox Searchlight Pictures, Ad Hominem Enterprises, Dune Entertainment, Little Blair Productions, Ingenious Film Partners. Distribution: Fox Searchlight. Role: Matt King

GRAVITY (Alfonso Cuarón, USA/UK, 2013)

Production: Warner Bros. Pictures, Esperanto Filmoj, Heyday Films. Distribution: Warner Bros. Role: Matt Kowalski

THE MONUMENTS MEN (George Clooney, USA/Germany, 2014)

Production: Fox 2000 Pictures, Columbia Pictures, Smokehouse, Obelisk Productions Ltd, Studio Babelsberg, Deutscher Filmförderfonds, Medienboard Berlin-Brandenburg, MDM. Distribution: Columbia. Role: Frank Stokes

TOMORROWLAND (Brad Bird, USA/Spain, 2015)

Production: Walt Disney Pictures, A113. Distribution: Disney. Role: Frank Walker

HAIL, CAESAR! (Joel and Ethan Coen, USA/UK/Japan, 2016)

Production: Universal Pictures, Working Title, Mike Zoss Productions. Distribution: Universal. Role: Baird Whitlock

MONEY MONSTER (Jodie Foster, USA, 2016)

Production: TriStar Pictures, Smokehouse, LStar Capital, Allegiance Theater. Distribution: Sony. Role: Lee Gates

Television

Chronologically ordered according to first transmission dates. With series where Clooney appeared in only an episode or episodes, the title is ordered according to the date of his first appearance.

CENTENNIAL (USA, 1978–9)
Production: Universal Television. Network: NBC. Role: uncredited
RIPTIDE (USA, 1984–6)
Production: Stephen J. Cannell Productions. Network: NBC. Role: Lenny Colwell (1984). 2/10/1984
STREET HAWK (USA, 1985)
Production: Universal Television. Network: ABC. Role: Kevin Stark. 11/1/1985
E/R (USA, 1984–5)
Production: Embassy Television. Network: CBS. Role: Ace. 12/12/1984
CRAZY LIKE A FOX (USA, 1984–6)
Production: Columbia Pictures Television, Wooly Mammoth Productions. Network: CBS. Role: uncredited. 31/3/1985
THE FACTS OF LIFE (USA, 1979–88)
Production: Embassy Pictures, TAT Communications Company. Network: NBC. Role: George Burnett (1985–7). 21/9/1985
HOTEL (USA, 1983–8)
Production: Aaron Spelling Productions. Network: ABC. Role: Nick Miller (1986). 29/1/1986
THROB (USA, 1986–8)
Production: Swany Inc., Procter & Gamble Productions, Taft Entertainment Television. Role: Rollo Moldonado (1986). 11/10/1986
COMBAT HIGH (USA, 1986)
Production: Frank von Zerneck Films, Lynch/Biller Productions. Network: NBC. Role: Major Biff Woods. 23/11/1986
HUNTER (USA, 1984–91)
Production: Stephen J. Cannell Productions. Network: NBC. Role: Matthew Winfield. 14/2/1987

MURDER, SHE WROTE (USA, 1984–96)

Production: Universal Television. Network: CBS. Role: Kip Howard.
15/3/1987

THE GOLDEN GIRLS (USA, 1985–92)

Production: Touchstone Television, Witt/Thomas/Harris Productions.
Network: NBC. Role: Bobby Hopkins (1987). 2/5/1987

BENNETT BROTHERS (USA, 1987)

Production: NBC. Network: NBC. Role: Tom Bennett. 22/7/1987

ROSEANNE (USA, 1988–97)

Production: Wind Dancer Productions, Carsey-Werner Company. Network:
ABC. Role: Booker Brooks (1988–9, 1991). 18/10/1988

SUNSET BEAT (USA, 1990, 1992)

Role: Chic Chesbro. 21/4/1990

KNIGHTS OF THE KITCHEN TABLE (USA, 1990)

Production: Ubu Productions. Role: Rick Stepjack

BABY TALK (USA, 1991–2)

Production: Columbia Pictures Television, Weinberger Company. Network:
ABC. Role: Joe (1991). 8/3/1991

REWRITE FOR MURDER (USA, 1991)

Production: Lorimar Television. Network: CBS. Role: Nick Bianco.
14/9/1991

SISTERS (USA, 1991–6)

Production: Cowlip Productions, Lorimar Productions, Warner Bros. Television.
Network: NBC. Role: Detective James Falconer (1992–3). 18/3/1992

BODIES OF EVIDENCE (USA, 1992–3)

Production: Roundelay Productions, James L. Conway Productions, Lorimar
Television. Network: CBS. Role: Detective Ryan Walker. 18/6/1992

JACK'S PLACE (USA, 1992–3)

Production: ABC Productions. Network: ABC. Role: Rick Logan (1992).
23/6/1992.

WITHOUT WARNING: TERROR IN THE TOWERS (USA, 1993)

Production: Melnicker Entertainment, Jurist Productions, Wilshire Court
Productions. Network: NBC. Role: Kevin Shea. 26/5/1993

THE BUILDING (USA, 1993)

Production: Bob and Alice Productions, Worldwide Pants Inc., CBS Entertainment Productions. Network: CBS. Role: Jim. 20/8/1993

ER (USA, 1994–2009)

Production: Amblin Television, Constant C Productions, John Wells Productions, Warner Bros. Television. Network: NBC. Role: Dr Doug Ross (1994–9, 2000, 2009)

FRIENDS (USA, 1994–2004)

Production: Warner Bros. Television, Bright/Kauffman/Crane Productions. Network: NBC. Role: Dr Michael Mitchell (1995). 23/2/1995

SOUTH PARK (USA, 1997–)

Production: Braniff Productions, Comedy Partners. Cable: Comedy Central. Voice: Sparky. 3/9/1997

MURPHY BROWN (USA, 1988–98)

Production: Shukovsky English Entertainment, Warner Bros. Television. Network: CBS. Role: Doctor #2. 18/5/1998

FAIL SAFE (Stephen Frears, USA, 2000)

Production: Maysville Pictures, Warner Bros. Television. Network: CBS. Role: Colonel Jack Grady. 9/4/2000

TEXT SANTA 2014 (Matt Hilton, UK, 2014)

Production: ITV Studios. Network: ITV. Role: Lord George Oceans Gravity, Marquis of Hollywood. 19/12/2014

Online

TOUCH OF EVIL (Alex Prager, USA, 2011) Production: *The New York Times*.

8 (Rob Reiner, USA, 2012). Production: American Foundation for Equal Rights, Broadway Impact. Distribution: YouTube. Role: David Boies

A VERY MURRAY CHRISTMAS (Sofia Coppola, USA, 2015). Production: American Zoetrope, Departed Productions, Jax Media, South Beach Productions. Distribution: Netflix. Role: himself

INDEX

List of Illustrations

Figures

Tables

PUBLISHED TITLES

Amitabh Bachchan *Sunny Singh*
Brigitte Bardot *Ginette Vincendeau*
Julie Christie *Melanie Bell*
Penelope Cruz *Ann Davies*
Madhuri Dixit *Nandana Bose*
Rock Hudson *John Mercer*
Deborah Kerr *Sarah Street*
Nicole Kidman *Pam Cook*
Tony Leung Chiu-Wai *Mark Gallagher*
James Mason *Sarah Thomas*
Carmen Miranda *Lisa Shaw*
Mickey Rourke *Keri Walsh*
Hanna Schygulla *Ulrike Sieglohr*
Barbara Stanwyck *Andrew Klevan*
Elizabeth Taylor *Susan Smith*
Denzel Washington *Cynthia Baron*
Natalie Wood *Rebecca Sullivan*
Star Studies *Martin Shingler*